UEA MA Crea[t]
Anthologies 2
Prose Fiction

University of East Anglia

egg b●x   University of East Anglia

UEA PROSE FICTION 2015

First published by Egg Box Publishing 2015

A CIP record for this book is available
from the British Library.

UEA PROSE FICTION 2015 is typeset in
Adobe Garamond. Titles are set in Mercury.

Cover photography from the photographic unit, UEA.

Printed and bound in the UK by Imprint Digital.

Designed and typeset by Sean Purdy.

Proofread by Sarah Gooderson.

Distributed by Central Books.

ISBN: 978-0-9932962-1-5

Acknowledgements

Thanks are due to the School of Literature, Drama and Creative Writing at UEA in partnership with Egg Box Publishing for making the UEA MA Creative Writing anthologies possible.

We'd also like to thank the following people:

Tiffany Atkinson, John Boyne, Andrew Cowan, Helen Cross, Giles Foden, Sarah Gooderson, Rachel Hore, Kathryn Hughes, Catrina Laskey, Bill Manhire, Jean McNeil, Natalie Mitchell, Jeremy Noel-Tod, Beatrice Poubeau, Rob Ritchie, Sophie Robinson, Helen Smith, Henry Sutton, Val Taylor, Ian Thomson, Steve Waters, Frances Wilson and Peter Womack.

Nathan Hamilton at Egg Box Publishing, and Sean Purdy.

Editorial team:

Rob Atkinson
Sohini Basak
Gill Blanchard
Jemma Carter
Joanna Graham
Alexis Kuzma
Elizabeth Lewis-Williams
Emma Victoria Miller
Molly Morris
Kayla Schmidt
Jade Tremblay
Chloe L Yeoh

CONTENTS

HELEN CROSS

Foreword

I N MY MA YEAR THERE WERE TWELVE PROSE WRITERS AND UEA'S FIRST intake of poets, just two of them. Most of us were young-ish escapees from the regular working world, and the course seemed a thrilling chance to be a freethinker again.

I had little to back up my excitement. I had written just a few short stories and a time-travelling first novel, half set on a fish dock in 1920s Hull and half in modern London.

At this time I was particularly snooty about genre, particularly the thriller, or any fat popular book, which I thought was made for the intellectually challenged. I was even more suspicious of plots and speech marks, though I was very keen on Northern dialect, the more authentically baffling the better.

Our leader, the poet Andrew Motion, known to us, partly for his calm manner, as The Lotion, took all this in his stride. He listened, gazed out of the window and studded our submissions with spidery 'eh?'s. He wanted clarity and focus. He said he liked prose that 'looked like water but tasted like gin.' He advised us to 'socialise' our writing. He tried to lure us away from wilful obscurity. He believed in us.

We also believed in one another, and, though our weekly group was homespun and often amateurish, it became a group of friends. There was an international divide: the Americans and the Canadians were notably sharper at workshopping than us Brits. They had articulate vocabulary to back up their hunches, and we listened for their comments most keenly.

Somehow over that year I got more drunkenly sure about myself as a writer. Confidence is always a trick. You can bring it out in yourself and in others. Fear and doubt kill it, just as surely as fun and friendship fertilise it.

Luckily we were completely spared agent visits and the cold dose of reality they often instil in relative innocents, until one final boozy party at Andrew's family home (and if that palace didn't inspire us to become successful writers nothing would). If I was ignorant about good writing when I started at UEA, I was still a complete blockhead about the publishing world when I left. We didn't ever talk about 'the market' and I understood the term 'quiet' to mean a thoughtful, tender story, probably written by a literary genius. All this helped my happiness enormously.

The course stopped with a shock: our all-night election party, which saw the end of eighteen years of Tory rule and the spectacular defeat of Michael Portillo. I was sure we were on the brink of a new age.

I left with no interest from agents, no distinction and a half-written second first novel, and immediately started work in Anglian Windows. It was a sleepy place where the secretaries whispered about their forthcoming weddings, and I was able to slip in the odd paragraph between memos about patio doors. Whatever surge of self-belief UEA had injected into me stayed long enough for me to finish the novel.

If I could sprinkle any magic over the wonderful writers collected here it would be for them not to worry about 'the market' and genre and whether their novel is 'quiet' or not. These need not be, simply *cannot* be, the writer's concern.

Anyway, it's not all gloom. It might never have been harder to sell a novel, but it's never been easier to publish one. The arts are still full of inspiring, creative people inventing new models of working together. Small publishers spring up each year, and there are many more literary magazines in which to share new work. The digital world has thrown up new markets and routes for writing, and it's still possible to make a living if you're resilient, crafty and adaptable.

And if these new writers can confidently make doing all that fun, they've cracked it.

Helen Cross

JEAN MCNEIL AND HENRY SUTTON

Introduction

'THE BRITISH CAN BE ODDLY PROVINCIAL IN OUTLOOK WHEN IT COMES
to literature.' This is a lately much-quoted statement from Marina
Warner, a judge for the 2015 Man Booker International Prize. Warner
was speaking of literature primarily in translation, but at UEA we often
discuss the connections and departures between cultures, experience,
resource, ethnicity, imagination, all adding to what might constitute a
writer's 'territory.'

The Creative Writing MA in Prose Fiction at UEA has become the
UK's most international such programme (as well as of course being
the oldest). Increasingly students from Asia, Africa and North America
are coming to Norwich to study, along with those from the UK and
elsewhere in the EU, especially Ireland. This diversity, aided by the wide
age range on the course, is reflected in the work you read here. A drug war
in São Paulo, a drought-afflicted homestead in 19th-century Queensland,
the aftermath of the assassination of Indira Gandhi in Delhi, a ballet
class in West London – the imaginative landscapes of our students' work
are constantly shifting, both for them and for us.

Behind these finished pieces lie a host of other projects that have
shaped their thinking and technical abilities, that have helped distil
visions. A change in perspective perhaps, structure, theme or voice.
These choices and decisions are the shadow play of literature, and for us
as tutors it is fascinating to work in this tenebrous realm, to enable and
enhance creative openings and opportunities. Our students surprise us
continuously, not only with the breadth of the settings, characterisation
and themes of their fiction, but often with their changes of direction,

reconsiderations, recastings. It's a truism that the general reader only reads what is on the page – what is finished. But there is an entire play taking place behind the dark velvet curtain that drops soundlessly in front of the finished work. As tutors, as with writers, we live backstage. We are witness to the rehearsals and sound checks that precede the material you read here. Influence can be subtle and unsubtle. What is perhaps more consistent is the aim of creating an environment that encourages and enables literary expression.

When this time of year rolls around course work is finished, the classroom already becoming a memory. Some academic pressure is off the students, but the real world beckons. As ever, we are amazed and surprised by the outcomes of another very intense year that we have had the privilege to preside over – a year of at times frantic reading and writing, of creative doubts and impasses, of breakthroughs and epiphanies. We move on, better readers, better writers, better equipped. We give you the class of 2015.

Jean McNeil
Henry Sutton
Co-convenors, Master's in Creative Writing: Prose Fiction

UEA MA Creative Writing Anthologies 2015: Prose Fiction

MIKE ADAMS

White Sands

'WHAT'S THAT YOU'RE READING ABOUT, BOY?' HE ASKS. THERE IS something dangerous about his look. 'Trials and tribulations?'

'It's just a book I borrowed from Louie. I'm not far yet,' I say.

'I read some when you was in the house, pretty heavy stuff.'

'Oh.' I wonder if he had found any of the sex scenes. Louie had marked a bunch of pages, and I'm shitting a brick thinking about how easy it would have been for him to turn to one.

He keeps looking down at me with that look in his eye, like he knows something big about me, or about the world, and isn't going to shake loose 'til he shows me what it is. I just sit there picking at clover in the grass hoping he'll forget I'm there. Finally, he shakes his head and mutters something to himself, and tips back his hat, softening. He looks out on the land miles past the barn and scratches his greying head.

'Goin' down the way later. Need to work that grullo horse Blankenship left. You get your act together, you can come.'

I nod and shove the thick book under my arm before running into the house. I cut through the dining room and into the kitchen to get a drink of milk, and Gramma and Uncle Ralph are inside shootin' the shit about some dump plans coming down their way, none too happy.

'And with all them toxins and whatnot goin' down into the water, who knows what'll end up in our well? And you know old Sam Grey isn't going to like it much, and he's got money.' Gramma gives Ralph a little wink, like she knows how it's all gonna work out.

'I don't reckon money comes into it much though, Mom. They wain't said—'

'How d'ya figure that? Them rich bigwigs from King Country are always getting into things.'

I look in the refrigerator and sigh. 'Gramma.'

'What, sweetheart?'

'Do you have two per cent milk? I don't like the red milk.'

'Red milk?'

'The red cap.'

'That's the good milk, sweetheart.' She walks over from where she'd been leaning on the countertop and gives me a wet kiss on the cheek. 'We don't like ours watered down.'

'OK.' I wipe my cheek to get rid of the slobber there and her eyebrows come together.

'Don't wipe my kiss off!'

'I'm not, Gramma. I'm rubbing it in.'

'All right, honey. That's OK then.'

Uncle Ralph laughs and slaps me on the back as I walk back out of the kitchen empty-handed. He follows me into the dining room and stands looking out of the big window. I stand next to him, glancing up at his face on my left before quickly looking back out at the yard in front and the dusty landscape that lies beyond it.

The yard is fenced and symmetrical, and there is a cement path down the middle that leads to some steps at the very edge of it, stopped by a metal gate. The steps cut steeply down through the terraced layer and end up far below, at the long drive that sweeps straight between the two pastures. The pasture on the right is empty right now, and the other holds the black stud, BJ. At the end, where the drive meets the gravel road, I can see the barn and the old outbuildings, where I've spent these summer weeks under the hot sun feeding the horses, the old donkey, Walter, and gathering eggs from the chickens. Gramma and Grampa used to have pigs they named after me and my sisters, but they'd probably eaten them a while back.

I look past the barn and out at the bluffs and coulees. There will be coyotes out there, and groundchucks. Badgers, probably, and other things I don't even know about. The whole place, far as I can see, looks dry. Tall brown and yellow-rust grasses are everywhere, and sagebrush and mustard plants. Those mustard plants will dry up around this time of summer and let go of the ground, and tumble around solo or in big group operations until they get caught on something or end up clumped together in one of those coulees, trapped between bluffs. They always taught us in school about the Missoula floods, and how the Scablands were made, but I can never imagine a flood big enough to scrape out such a crazy looking place as this – big boulders left stranded in the middle of nothing, hills topped with rock, lakes in the middle of the driest places I've ever seen.

'Your grampa's goin' out there later, you know.' Uncle Ralph looks down at me and smiles.

'I know, he said I could go with him.'

His smile stutters a little. 'Do what he says when you're out there, OK?'

'I will.' I wonder what's wrong with him, if maybe he's mad at me for going with Grampa when I usually go out with him.

I don't know how far away I am from the house, but it feels a fair distance. I'm on Jalapeño, Charmagne's gelding, and he's on Blankenship's grullo mare. We'd come through about ten gates and had passed through the last of Little Lakes a while back.

'Coming up on White Sands, pard,' he says. He leans in his saddle and takes out his Copenhagen Snus. 'How you liking that little cutting horse?'

'I like him fine. He's one of my favourites.'

'Well, good.' He has the lid off now, and he hooks a dip and sticks it in his bottom lip before closing the lid and standing in the stirrups to position the can in the worn place in the back pocket of his Wranglers. 'When we get up here, you'd better not let him roll over you. They're apt to do that.'

I nod. 'I know.'

The rippling hills give way to a steep wash with white sand on the near side. Grampa goes first, edging the grullo mare down the loose dirt and crumbling rock, and into the sand below, crossing the dry creek bed. I follow on Jalapeño, giving his flanks a nudge with my heels. I give him his head, loosening the reins, and he puts his muzzle to the ground, slowly stepping with stiff forelegs down the shifting dirt. When he steps into the sand, he stops and blows, little rivulets of sand grains running down the slope away from his breath. Before I realise it, he is dropping, and I just have time to lift my leg away from the slope as he leans onto it, and then I am standing, boots sinking into the sand, his body underneath me.

'Get outta there, goddamn it, get off 'eem! He'll roll on you!'

I stand frozen there, wondering whether I should give the gelding a kick to right him, or stop straddling him and step off into the sand.

Grampa's hollering is just flustering me, and I can't get my head straight from the panic. Eventually, I step off and stand at a distance while Jalapeño rolls, his cinch loosening, the saddle dropping low around his belly. When he finishes, he lurches upright and jerks his reins free of my hand and takes off down the creek bed.

I look over at Grampa and smile. 'I'm OK,' I say. 'Sorry.'

He silently rides the grullo over to me and looks down, and all I can see of his face is the black shadow that looms in front of the orange sun overhead. 'Wipe that smile off your face or I'll beat it off. I'll give you something to smile about – go fetch that horse.'

Mike Adams is a former US Air Force Staff Sergeant. He completed a BA at UEA before beginning the Creative Writing MA, and is working on a collection of interconnected short stories set in the American region known as the Channeled Scablands, located in the Inland Northwest.

PETER BLOXHAM

The Long Weekend

The following is the opening to a novelette.

1

HERE I AM. I AM STANDING ON THE SOFT, WET BANK OF A BEAUTIFUL clean loch, holding a bottle of twelve-year, single malt Scottish whisky and a glass. The air is crisp and fresh and cold; the sky is a beautiful, scalded pale blue. The icy wind whips inside my clothes and makes me feel alive and refreshed. I carefully place my bottle of whisky and my glass down on a mossy stump. I remove my boots and my socks and roll my trousers up to my knees. I pick up my whisky and wade carefully into the clear water; the coldness sends a wave of energy through my legs and into my spine. I focus very carefully on directing the rush of energy into a positive visualisation of myself.

'I can achieve. I can be happy. I am the person I want to be,' I say to myself quietly. The soft mud feels rich and luxurious as it gives way to my weight and swallows up my feet. A large piece of ice floats near to me; I scoop it into my glass and pour myself a generous measure of this wonderful, golden single malt. I take a nice big, peaty swallow and feel the warmth travel down my throat and into my stomach. On the far bank of the loch I can see a huge, proud stag with magnificent antlers. He turns his head and stares at me. I raise my glass to him; he snorts at me in respect, steam billowing from his wild, beautiful nostrils.

Life is like this, I think to myself and I feel enormously contented. I drain my glass and wade out of the water; I pick up my shoes and socks. My feet and calves are pink. I walk just a few yards back to the guest house: an appealing, cosy little building made of stone and slate. I enter the lounge and feel the soft red carpet on my bare feet and the warmth from the real log fire and I ask for two pints of ale and two venison steaks with potatoes, served medium rare. I ask for them to be sent upstairs to our room. The man behind the bar says something friendly in his charming Scottish accent.

I climb the stairs to our room and open the door, and Charlotte is there sitting in the big, ornate armchair made from rich, stained oak with her lovely dark hair in curls, and her lips are red and she's wearing some really fantastic-looking lacy lingerie that I didn't even know she'd brought; she looks very sexy in a very tasteful way.

And she has her right hand inside of her underwear and it's moving very gently and slowly and she looks up at me.

And I say, 'I ordered us venison.'

She says something positive, indicates that she is happy with this choice I have made, that it's good that I have taken the initiative to order us venison and that she feels happy.

As I'm having sex with Charlotte, I am able to see through the window and take in the vast unspoiled expanse of heather and fern and pine and the shining water and clear sky and light mist and a mountain, and my muscles fix and so do hers and we just explode with love and passion and pleasure.

Afterwards Charlotte is eating her venison with some sort of primal hunger, just completely unashamed and natural, with meat juice on her chin, and she looks at me and puts her hand on my shoulder and says, 'Thank you, I am so incredibly satisfied.'

And this will be our long weekend in Scotland and everything will be fine. And it will never really end because we will capture the positivity and the clarity and the hopefulness, and take it home with us and remember how to be happy together again.

I am driving us in the car to Scotland. I have the guest house set on Google Maps. Charlotte has fallen asleep in the passenger seat with her phone in her hand. A white Audi cuts across two lanes and forces me to apply the brakes.

Bastard.

2

It is taking a lot longer to get to Scotland than I thought it would. I have been driving for five hours. About an hour ago I passed Leeds. I think I am near Durham. None of these places is as far north as I had thought. I am very tired; I badly need to piss. I recently missed the service station that I had been planning to use for twenty miles. I swore rapidly and passionately but very quietly. I hit the steering wheel angrily but gently, to avoid waking up Charlotte.

Charlotte has been asleep for four hours. If she wakes up she will want to know how close we are; we are not as close as we should be. She will want to know how much longer and I will get the answer wrong. She will later remind me of how wrong my answer was. She will offer to drive, I will say no. I am going to get us there without any hitches. I am going to drive all the way.

Her friends will text her to ask how the weekend away is going:

'Hey, how's the weekend away going? x'

'So lovely! He drove us all the way without any hitches whatsoever! x'

Or better yet, 'Hey hey, how's the big weekend away going? d x x'

'Hi David, please stop texting me and fuck off now, please. I'm having a fantastic time in Scotland with my boyfriend who I am in love with. You are a creepy dickhead and we are not friends, stop trying to get in my pants. x'

The sun has gone down; I am driving in the twilight. I am hungry and thirsty. When we get to a service station I will take a long, luxurious piss. I will have a bottle of water from WHSmith and a coffee from Costa or Nero or Starbucks or whatever they have and hopefully a fast food cheeseburger. I think about the cool water flowing into my mouth, rinsing my sticky tongue, priming my stomach for the delicious cheeseburger. The petrol seems to be lasting better than I thought it would anyway, which is a sign that everything is going brilliantly.

I hope that the guest house is easy to find from the main road. I turn on Radio 4 very quietly.

Charlotte shifts in the passenger seat.

'Ugh. Sorry,' she says. 'I must've been really tired. How close are we?'

3

Charlotte and I are sitting in a motorway services branch of Costa. The chairs are bolted to the ground. I am drinking an enormous americano with milk. Charlotte is drinking an enormous americano without milk. She is reading Twitter on her white iPhone.

The music playing in Costa is an Amy Winehouse song; it's one that I quite like. It has a jazzy little piano ditty and jittery drum beat and Amy is laying it on nice and thick as usual, and there's that brass that seemed to go everywhere with her for a while. I think about saying 'Classic Winehouse' and making Charlotte laugh.

I'm ninety-three per cent certain that we're going the right way. I am trying not to think about the possibility that Google Maps is telling me the wrong way, or that I have somehow failed to follow Google Maps properly, or that Google Maps actually has the wrong guest house set as the destination and has matched my keywords to a different place that is either fully booked or too expensive. My iPhone battery has been shit recently (I am due an upgrade in three months). This means that I can't really afford to have the GPS on constantly. I can only check where I am occasionally. I have to keep resetting the Google Maps app for some reason; I keep pressing the wrong thing and losing where I am. If my battery dies after I leave the motorway I am completely fucked.

The amount of caffeine in my absurdly large coffee is giving me anxiety. I take a deep breath and puff my cheeks out. Chill out, I think. I breathe out slowly. Charlotte has placed her phone face down on the table and is looking out at the car park.

'You OK?' she says without looking at me.

'Yep,' I say. 'Pretty happy with how it's going. Very happy actually.' Charlotte must remain in a good mood. Charlotte must have the longest ever uninterrupted period of good mood that she has ever had. She must be shielded from all negativity. She will associate this incredible period of unbroken good mood, as facilitated by me, with being in my company. This is the same thing as love. She will romanticise this period of her life, even this service station, even this horrible, expensive coffee. She will romanticise me. After I'm dead, she'll tell our great-grandchildren how lovely I was, tell them about this weekend, mention my breezy, self-assured, friendly, charming attitude and how consistently attractive I always was to her.

Three days ago I told Charlotte that I loved her – nothing unusual, just a routine, maybe slightly overused 'I love you.' She didn't say it back. I'm fairly sure that she just didn't hear me; I think that's possible. She was standing maybe four feet away, halfway through the door, about to turn around. Anyway, you can't really repeat yourself in that situation. I've been a bit afraid to say 'I love you' since. She hasn't said it either. Maybe it's good. Taking a break from that phrase is good for couples. That's probably the sort of shit people get paid to write in *Cosmopolitan* or whatever, but it's probably true. You can't just keep hammering away with that phrase; you need to take a break from it. When we say it again, we'll have gained a new respect for saying it, a new pleasure. We'll say it maybe once every couple of weeks and really mean it.

'What was the sigh for? You OK?' Charlotte is sipping her coffee.

'Yeah, yeah, totally fine,' I say, accidentally sort of sighing.

'Hey beardy, come on.' Charlotte uses a temporary pet name for me while I have a beard. I'm pretty sure Charlotte is attracted to men with beards: men with thick arms and body hair who can plane wood or whatever, who smell of damp and charcoal and wood-smoke and don't say much and can pick her up in one thick calloused hand and are quitting their job at the sawmill to move to Tokyo and study Kawakami Hajime for a PhD or whatever.

I can grow a pretty good beard.

Charlotte is smirking at me. She is a very attractive woman. She is the only woman this attractive who will ever go out with me. She is my only chance to be loved by a nice person who is intelligent, interesting, has talents, is genuinely funny and is also somehow an attractive woman. She's an anomaly, a freak. There is no way I can ever, ever let her go.

If I say that nothing is wrong, I run the risk of a) trying her patience and/or b) making her think that I am holding back my concerns about being able to drive us successfully to Scotland without any hitches. I need a diversion, something to dismiss.

'Oh... it's just...' I'm not sure what I'm going to say. I think for a moment. 'It's just I can't believe that Amy Winehouse is dead.'

The Amy Winehouse song is finished. Costa is now playing Fleetwood Mac.

Charlotte looks at me carefully.

'Yep. It's sad,' she says.

I nod and look out at the car park. I really want to get going. 'Yeah,' I say. 'Such a waste. Such a complete waste.'

Peter Bloxham is based in London. He is interested in humour, surrealism and sentimentality. He is writing a novel about a young man who discovers that he is a genetic copy of Martin Amis. More of his writing is available at peterbloxham. tumblr.com and @ohgodohgod.

PAULA COCOZZA

Fox

SHE HAD ENTERED HIS WORLD. WHEN SHE WALKED TO THE STATION on Monday morning, his hot blast of musk enveloped her as she passed her front railings. The smell rose again at the new builds at the end of her street, out on the main road, and at the fringe of the park. It hit her intermittently, as if she were passing through chambers of scent. The whole neighbourhood was his castle, all the roads and houses and gardens portions of some enormous floor plan to which she now held the key. How long had it been here, this invisible, pungent architecture? Had she simply failed to notice it – or was the first time she saw him the day he moved into the area? Almost without looking, Mary spotted the signs of him, the tidy droppings by a lamppost. As she left the park and turned towards Haggerston station, a gang of crows dispersed over the rooftops with a sudden cawing, and she imagined him moving below them, his shoulders dropped and rolling, belly dusting the ground.

On Monday evening, the fox appeared in her garden five minutes after she got home, nudged at the corner of the blanket where she lay, then sat upright on the lawn a short way off. They eyed each other cautiously, as if they both understood that their relationship was entering a new phase. On Tuesday she left work half an hour earlier than Monday, and there he was again, strolling through the long grass. He sat a little closer this time, measuring his advances with exactitude. She watched his claws extending and retracting in the dry earth of the thinning lawn, toying with the invisible string that divided his space from hers.

And so the week went on. Without either of them needing to say, they settled into a routine: she would come outside, and he would appear.

It made no difference what time she unlocked the back door. From the woods, he heard her footsteps, or caught her cologne. He seemed to know her movements, to have a superhuman sense of her whereabouts, no matter how she tested him with small variations to her timing, or how quietly she drew back the lock and tiptoed outside. The fox knew more about her comings and goings than her mother, her neighbours, and Dawn put together, and Dawn sat opposite her for eight hours a day (eight hours in theory). It said a great deal about how little people noticed Mary that she could slip out of the office unseen. Yet she found it impossible to re-enter her own home without being met.

On Wednesday, after he'd sprung his exit over her back wall, she left the blanket out in the garden. The sky had forgotten how to rain. And the fox was no longer a threat. He was encroaching on her life the way any new relationship encroaches, and she shifted over to make space for him. The blanket was an open invitation, their sofa in front of the telly, the place where they met and crashed at the end of the day. Well, it was the end of her day – perhaps only the start of his. She knew he slept on the rug while she was at work, because it bristled with his smoky tang.

On Thursday, she arrived back from the office an hour earlier than Wednesday. The edges of the blanket curled upwards in the sun and this time when he walked down the lawn to meet her, he did not stop, but slipped his snout beneath a frayed corner. Her limbs stiffened. She was lying on her stomach, but she tilted fractionally to see the squares of plaid ruck and crumple into new shapes over his head. He knew she was watching, because he withdrew his muzzle from under the blanket and looked straight at her, purpose warming his amber eyes. A thread snapped as his paw snagged the rug. He was nosing on top of it now; his snout led him towards her. His ear tipped forward, spiking the edge of her vision. Mary froze. Would he stop sniffing, stop walking, when he reached her? But his legs folded beneath him right where he stood and they lay side by side on their bellies, looking at the trees, watching the shadow of a bee crawl across a low-hanging hazel leaf, trawling veins with its antennae. The hard part was done. They had got here, together at last. Now they could relax, lie in the sun and talk.

His tail thumped the hot fleece they lay on. Relax? If only! Whiskers flickered. Ears perked at the tangle of sounds. The human hummed and the great tits squeaked and fussed in the hazel, and a woodlouse drummed its din of iron feet along a fallen leaf. Poor attempt at discretion.

He atomised some scent from the notch in his tail. A formality. They all knew he was there. The woodlouse clumped across the middle vein of its leaf and – the leaf tipped. Woodlouse upside-down! Little legs waggling fascinatingly. Stretching, straining, leaning, this way, that way, this way…

His snout was swaying, watching something. It was not a thought she could share with any person she knew, but Mary believed, from the way his muzzle was bobbing in excitement, the happy beat of his tail on the blanket, that he enjoyed the sound of her voice. He was so easy to talk to. He seemed to know what she wanted. The thing was, she had stuck to her guns with Mark. But she'd never said, never decided, that she wanted to be on her own. It was his ultimatum, her decision. Technically, that meant she had dumped him, which served him right for being so controlling. But all she had held on to was the freedom not to have a baby. Now there was no one to have a baby with anyway. It was a pointless victory. And here was Mark again. Turned up just around the corner. Checking she was safe. Living somewhere near, but refusing to say where. 'I bet you know,' she said, turning to the fox. 'Have you seen him? Is he living with someone else?' If he knew Mark, if Mark lived within his territory, maybe he went through Mark's bin. A bin was very revealing. She looked at the fox, the code that kept unlocking things. 'What are you crunching on?' she said. Thank God for the house. This house was all she had.

This nice den.

He looked around for another. Snappy things with a little chew inside. Not much effort to. Especially if they were in easy—

Her voice soothed him, she could see by the way he tucked his snout under the bushy hairs of his tail and his eyes shrank to a wet seam. But his ears never slept. She watched them, flickering and twitching as she chatted, their minute movements like an electronic readout of her tenor/base balance. Up, down, down, up. Or twisting right round when she heard the clatter of dinner things next door, then when Eric and George called again and again for their cat. 'Tiggy! Tiggy Tig-Tig!' They were large ears, and their size told a truth about him: he was an excellent listener. It occurred to her that – contrary to Mark's evaluation – she might be an excellent communicator. All she had needed was the chance to be one.

Just once her fox stayed still for so long while she was talking, she thought he had fallen asleep. She coughed sharply, and the near ear turned frontally to face her. She saw the line of dark hair inside, a narrow black ovoid, as if his ears had pupils too, and through them he saw and heard her in unison. He resettled himself, folded his haunches into a crouch beneath his rump. Even lying down like this, his legs never looked fully relaxed, but already committed to their next move, whatever the next move might be. They pulsed with intention, the quickness of his instinct. And when it was time for him to go – he decided this – he stood in one fluid motion. Black legs steeped in stealth, he rippled his way to the far corner of the garden. She had begun to wonder if he had a secret transportation station tucked away in the tiny space between her shed and the neighbouring fence.

On Friday, Mary was filling the kettle, ready to wash down her first pill. The blast of water filled her ears and drowned all the words there. When she turned around, he was watching her. All four feet were inside, and the kitchen had shrunk. Her mouth opened, but the words were dry. Her stomach muscles tightened as she swallowed the jolt of surprise. Get a grip, she thought. This is the natural next step.

They had been getting to know each other for a few weeks now. Almost a month. Of course he'd want to see where she lived. How else was he going to find out more about her? Don't be scared, she told herself. Sometimes taking control means surprising yourself, disobeying the familiar instincts, thwarting the same old you, the same old you's perennial attraction to the same old you's typical decisions. She had to learn to open up. It was like living in confinement, inside this head. She felt a fierce retaliation against the way her world had narrowed. Tonight she would not surrender to her lonely Monday night, Tuesday night, every-night lock-in. Tonight was going to be different.

'OK,' she said, stepping aside with a flourish. 'Be my guest.'

He nodded.

It was so easy. One simple decision, and life was a new place.

He sniffed at his feet. He lifted his muzzle and dropped it again a few inches off. His nose dabbed the ground, trying to filter the right signals through the interference. The smells came so faint. An electric hum zigzagged from the floor, through his claws, up to his shins. He could feel it juddering his knee joints. Very mixed messages. He adjusted his paws. New ground. Take it one twitch at a time. Foxes all around. Small ones and big ones. Whole ones and parts of ones. Pairs of eyes. Flashes of white from patches of chest. He was reluctant to go further in. One ear inclined.

The earth was humming, the strange calls of what? He slung his snout low and high, but not one of these foxes had scent. His own scent was the only fox scent. That was good. He pulled up his tail and released some more. Better. It was coming through strongly now. His claws curled into the floor, and the floor clung to his claw. To get rid of the stickiness, he lifted a leg and kept lifting it until the floor let go.

'Sorry,' she said. 'I'm planning to replace the lino.' Then, seeing him hesitate, she gestured further into the house. 'Come on, this way.' He was in her world now. He was everywhere in this room. She could see him in the sheen of the bin, the silvery surround of the oven, the glint of the toaster and kettle. One by one, all those mirrors emptied themselves of him and darkened. He was on the move. His paws click-clacked warmly down the wooden floorboards of the hall towards the lounge. Mary felt as good as if she had let some second self out of the cage.

Paula Cocozza is a staff writer at *The Guardian*. She is the 2013/14 recipient of the David Higham Award. *Fox* is an edited extract from her first novel-length fiction. Set in contemporary east London, it's the story of one woman's obsession with a fox.

ABBY ERWIN

What I Started

Extract from a novel.

W E LIE IN THE SCRUBBY GRASS AT THE BOTTOM OF THE GARDEN, LIZZIE on her back with her head in the shade of a rhubarb leaf, me on my stomach, watching columns of ants trickle around the roots of Grandma's hydrangea bush. Since we couldn't find any lollies in the freezer, I bashed some ice cubes out of their tray instead, and now we're sucking their cold water from the gaps between our fingers.

Lizzie sighs, hard, and I can see all her ribs rising and falling through the thin cotton of her top. 'This is pathetic.'

'What is?' I say, without raising my chin from the itchy patch of lawn it's pressed against.

'We are. This day. This summer. It's like a million degrees, and everyone is at the beach, or having sex, probably, and we're in Loserville, Isle of Wight, eating ice cubes.' She spits hers out onto the grass between us, a pale, half-melted moon.

My back is boiling so I roll over and expose the slope of my belly to the sun. I'm annoyed by her implication: that we're losers, that I'm a loser. Of course, I know it's true – I'm not an idiot – but it's not like she has anything better to do. If it weren't for me, she'd be spending all day at home playing PlayStation with her dad.

'I mean, why don't we just go to the beach?' she whines. 'I could get my mum to drive us to Ventnor. Then at least in September I'd have something to say when people ask me what I did this summer.'

I don't know who she thinks is going to be interested. 'We can't go to the beach. You know who hangs out there? Ella and her friends. Can you imagine, me in a swimsuit, and Jamie Gilbert? It'd be like wrapping my naked body in bacon and climbing into a tank of piranhas.'

'I bet Ella's having an amazing time. Sneaking out and getting drunk and kissing boys. That's what summers are meant to be like. We're wasting our youth!' Lizzie practically wails.

'Can we not talk about Ella?' The thought of my sister ties my stomach into sick, angry knots. When I think about what happened on Monday I have to fight back the urge to dig a hole in Grandma's floral border and hibernate there for the rest of the summer, maybe forever.

'At least her life's interesting.'

More interesting than you realise, I think. The thought of what I saw last night is nagging at me, buzzing round my head like a fat, biting fly. And because I'm bored, because I can't think of anything else to say or do, I tell Lizzie: 'I saw her last night, you know. With a man.'

'So?'

'As in, a man, not a boy. Old.'

'Really? Who?' She sits up, propping herself on her elbows behind her.

'I dunno, Lizzie, I don't know any men. But he was properly old, like forty maybe. He dropped her off on our road really late last night.'

'What were they doing?'

'Hugging, I guess? Maybe kissing.'

'Ugh, that's so gross,' she says with delighted disgust. 'I can't believe she's letting some old guy hump her. She's so pretty.'

'What?' The melted ice cube I swallowed earlier feels like it's re-freezing inside me, a cold hard brick rising in my throat. 'You don't think they're doing it, do you?'

'Duh. What other explanation could there possibly be?'

'God, you're so sick-minded. There's plenty of other things that could be going on.'

Lizzie's shaking her head at me and smiling in that infuriating way that she does when she thinks I'm being particularly babyish and she's being particularly grown-up. 'Of course she is. She might not want to, but she knows she has to if she wants him to be interested in her. That's how it works. What else would a man that age want with her?'

I feel sick now, my stomach fizzing with something sour and horrible. 'That's awful.'

'That's men for you,' says Lizzie, head bobbling sympathetically. 'Besides, she probably deserves it, after what she did to you.'

I weave my fingers through the grass and pull it up by the roots in handfuls. I know Lizzie's probably talking shit, but there's something inside me, something dark and ugly, that wants to find out more. 'I don't believe you.'

'Bet you I can prove it. Come on, she's at work all day, isn't she? We can start with your room.' She's pulling herself to her feet, an excited pink spot blooming on each cheekbone.

I stand and follow her through to the gloom of the house, because what else am I going to do? Somewhere in that deep, dark part of myself, I'm starting to form a plan. If we find what we're looking for, maybe there's some way I can use it against Ella. Maybe I can do to her what she did to me – rip her world to shreds.

'What exactly are we looking for?' I ask.

We stand in the space between Ella's bed and mine. Grandma swept through here already this morning, pulling the duvets straight and clearing dirty mugs from the bedside tables, sucking up long golden strands of Ella's hair with the hungry mouth of her hoover. She poked her head round the door just now and said she's going over the road to see her friend Pat, the one who has to sleep in her armchair since she broke her hip and can't climb the stairs up to bed anymore. Grandma likes to go and fuss around her, make her cups of tea and plump her cushions. I think she just likes having a captive audience. So she should be out of our way for a while, but still my breath keeps catching in my throat, my eyes watching the handle of the closed bedroom door for any flicker of movement.

Lizzie sits down on Ella's bed and slides her hand under the pillow. She pulls out Ella's nightie, crushed into a crumpled disc, and drops it onto the floor. Then she pulls the covers off, balling them up at the foot of the bed.

'What are you doing?' I hiss. 'Don't make such a mess!'

'Chill out, I'll put it all back when I'm done.' Lizzie puts her face to the mattress and sniffs.

'What are you checking for?'

'Sex smell.'

'What? As though you'd be able to tell.'

'I can too. My mum and dad used to stink of it on Sunday mornings, before they stopped sleeping in the same room.'

'Well, she's not going to be doing it here, is she? I share a room with her, you moron.'

'Fine.' Lizzie tosses the duvet back onto the bed, although without the geometric precision Grandma arranged it with earlier. I flop over and try to straighten things out while she moves on to Ella's wardrobe. 'Which one's her knicker drawer?'

'God, you really are a lezzie, aren't you?'

She turns to me with her cheeks blazing. 'People hide things in their knicker drawer, Thea. I'm not doing this because I enjoy it.'

I sigh. 'It's the second one down.'

She pulls out the entire drawer and empties it onto the bed. Bras and knickers everywhere: little lacy thongs, satin push-up bras, stretched-out boyshorts with the days of the week on them. Lizzie rummages through them delicately, using the tips of her fingers like tweezers. 'Hmm. Well, she definitely has some sexy stuff in here,' she says, looping her pinkie through the flossy ribbon of a purple thong and holding it up for inspection.

'That doesn't mean anything,' I say, trying to slide the drawer back onto its runners, straining my ears for the click of the lock that will signal Grandma's return. Or even worse, Ella's.

'Not necessarily,' says Lizzie, holding her nose up to the purple satin and having a good sniff. 'But it's a start.'

I look at the scraps of silky cloth laid out on the bed and think of my big pale mollusc body forced into something like that, the string of the thong lost somewhere up my enormous bum. It's too depressing to contemplate.

Lizzie pockets the purple thong. 'What's that for?' I ask.

'DNA testing,' she says.

'Rubbish.'

She considers a light blue bra, holding it up against her skinny chest. 'Don't just stand there, give me a hand.'

'I don't think my sense of smell's as good as yours.'

'I mean, have a look through some of her other stuff.'

'Like what? You're the mastermind here.'

'Does Ella keep a diary?' Lizzie asks.

'She used to. I don't think she does anymore.'

I'd spent many empty afternoons lying on her bed on my stomach, leafing through entries that said stuff like, 'Got the best mark in maths today, haha, bet Chloe was gutted I did better than her,' and 'I HATE HATE HATE THEM!!! (By them of course I mean my stupid family, especially fat crybaby Thea.)' But as far as I know she lost interest in it over the last couple of years.

'Where did she used to keep it?' Lizzie's throwing fistfuls of pants back into the drawer. It looks a mess. No way is Ella not going to notice. I reach past her and try to fold some of them, smoothing them flat with sweaty palms.

'Top bedside drawer.'

'Have a look, then.' She's flicking through the clothes on hangers now, reaching out and scrabbling about at the back of the wardrobe as though she's hoping to find Narnia.

The top drawer of Ella's bedside table is full of make-up, dozens of little bottles and compacts all scattered in haphazard layers. Something's leaked at some point and it's left a layer of grease and powder that comes away on my fingers. I don't know how she has so much; she's always going on about how little pocket money we get and how her clothes are so much worse than all the other girls' in her year.

Lizzie's behind me, chin perched on my shoulder like a parrot. 'Anything?'

'Nah, just a load of lipstick and stuff.'

She reaches over me and picks up a gold tube. 'Where did she get all this? It looks expensive.'

'I dunno, Boots?'

'No way can she afford to get all this stuff for herself. Either she's nicking it, or someone's buying it for her.'

In the bottom drawer we find a box of tampons, which makes Lizzie laugh hysterically for some reason.

'How does it go in?' Lizzie makes a little hole with her fist and tries to shove the cardboard tube in sideways. 'There's so many parts!'

'There's instructions in the box,' I say. Any reminder of periods is a painful thing for me at the moment, which luckily Lizzie realises and stops trying to talk me into going to the bathroom to try one out.

Lizzie pockets the unwrapped tampon as well because we don't know what else to do with it and Ella might spot it in the waste paper basket. The other things in the drawer are: some charms off a broken bracelet, a fluffy hot water bottle, a few gritty coins and a white plastic box that a mobile phone came in. Hardly incriminating stuff.

'I'm hungry,' I say, starting to close the drawer. 'You want some lunch?'

'Hang on.' She picks up the box. 'Why's she kept this?' She takes the lid off and tips it out onto the bed.

Multicoloured foil squares scatter on the top of the duvet. With their zigzag edges and slight bulge in the middle they look a little like ravioli, and my stomach rumbles. 'What are those?'

Lizzie holds one of them up and reads the words off the wrapper: 'Durex, one latex condom.' She looks at me with triumph flashing in her eyes. 'See? She's totally doing it.'

Abby Erwin was born in Germany and grew up in India. She has lived in Norwich since 2010 and is currently working on a novel as well as a collection of short stories.

Ice Cream

THE ICE CREAM WAS THE COLOUR OF LITTLE GIRLS' DREAMS. I POKED my tongue into it like an insult and flicked a stream of strawberry cream into my mouth. I felt it trickle coolly down the inside of my throat, like the inversion of drinking whisky. And thicker – more sticky and viscous. The coolness of it running down the dark tunnels inside me made me alive to the fact that I had a body, aware of its heat; the difference between what was on the inside and what was on the outside. I caught some drips that were leaking down the skin of the cone on the tip of my tongue, and then looked up. You were watching me and I assumed you were thinking of blowjobs. I checked the crotch of your khaki pants for signs. The sun was beating so hard that I could smell the heat of my skin. Ripe freckles were bursting on my bronzed shoulders. I stood up straight, cocked my head to one side and smiled. It looked like I was looking into your eyes but I wasn't; I was checking myself out in your sunglasses. That's all I was that summer. Surface and reflection. I had a cherry stain tint on my lips, a white vest top beneath my dungaree shorts and you: I was trying myself out to see how I fit. I was starting to like the fit. But I was young; this was only act one. Its rehearsal.

'So you gonna show me where you live or what?' I said.

We'd crossed paths that day and you'd 'Charmed' me. You were Dan, 28, on my Happn, but then what did that mean? I was Amber, 21, on yours. The good thing about being tall is people believe you're older than you really are. The twenty-one was audacious though. I could have raised my age to eighteen and still been able to get into clubs; I could have pumped it up to sixteen if I was worried about guys thinking I wasn't legal, but I'd gone way over and above, a massive seven years, a big fat extra 50 per cent on my life. I was pushing my luck but I liked pushing luck.

We were about an hour and a half into what I guess would be described as a first date if first dates existed anymore; lunch at a deli on Newman Street, and we'd just started abusing these ice creams, so it might have seemed a bit forward, asking to go back to your flat already, but what did I know? I thought this was how it was done. It was Sunday afternoon and I wanted this down by Monday morning. I imagined the looks on the other girls' faces as I told them while we bundled through the playground doors towards registration. *Did it hurt? Was it big?* they'd ask. *Fucking enormous*, I'd say. *I thought he was gonna split me in two.*

You shifted your weight to your other foot. 'My flatmate will be back at four,' you said and I think your cheeks blushed but it could have been sunburn.

I shrugged.

He pushed it in and I gasped. I had figured I didn't have a hymen left from all the horse riding I'd done as a kid but maybe I had after all. I styled it out as a moan, exhaling a quivery sigh and he didn't seem to notice the difference. For a few strokes it felt uncomfortable, physically, like he was scratching a space inside me that didn't have an itch but things kind of loosened up and gradually it began to feel less like unwanted friction. It was never quite pain although it wasn't like pleasure either. It wasn't even close.

I clung to his back for want of a better thing to do with my hands and his skin felt clammy and a little squidgy. He wasn't fat but he could do with toning up. I looked over his shoulder, which was easy to do because he was boring his head into my neck. I focused on the landscape of his skin, peachy mountains with pearls of sweat rising up through the pores, sitting beadlike, perfect orbs, little see-through crystal globes on the back of his shoulders. *He's got the whole world in his hands, he's got the whole wide world in his hands* started to play in my head, which even I thought was probably pretty inappropriate, thinking of Jesus at that time. We'd sung that in assembly at primary school, sitting cross-legged on the floor with the white pages of our hymn book spread wide open. For a moment I wondered if the seven-year-old me had imagined that this was how it would turn out. I decided probably not but I wasn't sad about it. I just figured that at that age we still believed in love and Disney. I was glad to be done with that. I killed the song by re-engaging with his back. He had a few wisps of back hair, fine but unexpectedly long and straight, growing downwards on the blades of his shoulders. A few I could cope with – I was glad it wasn't a full pelt – but at the same time it made me feel sorry for him, like he was slightly pathetic. The image of me sitting on the floor cross-legged in assembly in my primary school tunic, white tights and buckle shoes came back into my head, along with the face of my old headmistress, with her tight black curls, sixty-year-old sagging cheeks and marionette lines, reading the bible story about the camel. It wasn't actually about a camel, it was the one about it being easier for a camel to pass through the eye of the needle than a rich man to enter the kingdom of heaven, but the image of the camel was such a powerful one that it had eclipsed the meaning of the story in my mind and every time I heard or remembered the story I couldn't picture the man, I could only envision a full-sized camel trying to squeeze through the eye of a needle. This image was always set against the backdrop of a desert and a throbbing blue sky with a high sun whose rays struck the needle and made it glisten and shine (like the fake 'ping' sparkles that come off the teeth of the models in the whitening toothpaste ads). I wondered if that was how it had felt for his dick: camel-like, squeezing through my fleshy slit.

He was still plunging up and down inside me and I thought this was a good opportunity to practise some moves, so I clawed my fingernails down his back like I was really into it and super wild like a sex tiger. I swear I felt him scrunch his eyebrows together like I was doing something weird so I stopped and tried to remember something else from all the how-to-be-amazing-at-fucking books I'd read. I tried shifting to the right, but I was pinned by his weight so I didn't get far. I leaned awkwardly and stretched my arm, straining to reach to cup his balls but given my arm was shorter than the length of his body, it didn't seem possible and I couldn't work out how to navigate the tangle of sweaty limbs. I remembered the bit about using your pelvic floor muscles so I started squeezing, clenching and releasing, which made him feel bigger inside me and as if I had clamped his dick in a vice, like the ones we use in DT class.

I practised my panting. Those desperate 'ooooh ooooh ooooh' sounds, sucking air between my teeth and biting my bottom lip like they do on YouPorn and he exploded into an epileptic fit of spasms and Tourette's. 'Fuck, shit, you fucking slut…'

I was stunned: I thought men were mute throughout, that it was just the women who were supposed to make noises. I felt like I'd accessed a rare Aladdin's cave; he was out of control on me, and with a final exclamatory grunt, he collapsed.

As soon as he was done, my body spat him out. There was a sound of a whoopee cushion, a liquid uncorking, and it felt like ejecting a slug. He rolled off me onto his back, cradled his head in the cage of his hands and closed his eyes.

I lifted the duvet – was hit by the smell of musky, fishy fluids – peered under and there it was: a cherry burst all over his navy sheets. I was pleased about the navy; the blood looked less accusatory against the darkness.

'Sorry, I think I've come onto my period,' I said.

I didn't know if the circular pool was what coming onto your period during sex looked like but who knows, maybe neither did he because he ducked his head under the duvet and said, 'No worries. I needed to wash the sheets today anyway.'

I dragged my bum along the sheet as I manoeuvred to the side of the bed, wiping myself clean. I was slimy all around my crotch and the crack of my bum. I retrieved my thong from the mangy carpeted floor and slipped it on. The crotch was soggy and the wetness was cold. It felt wrong, like inhabiting a past that no longer suited the present. But as I stood up and clamped my legs together I realised I was puffy and raw, so the coolness was partially soothing. His cum was starting to burn; little stabbing throbs were blooming inside me as if he'd ejaculated a sackful of thorns.

'You can stay a bit longer if you want,' he said to my turned back.

All I wanted was to be out of the flat: out of the cold, dark cave and back in the heat of the sun, feeling it pounding my skin, drying me out, turning me brown.

'Can't,' I said, 'I've got a big presentation tomorrow I need to prepare for.' I imagined Lauren's and Chloe's faces as they listened to me, me walking between them on the way to class, salacious seeds of wisdom spilling from my lips and growing into gossip. By lunchtime the whole year would know. There'd be analysis as knives were slipped into jacket potatoes, steam rising from their soft insides like whispers that would accompany me as I walked by. By the end of the day, people in other years might know; it might spread all the way to the boys in year eleven who sat at the back of the bus.

As I clipped my dungarees up he said, 'So… we should do this again.'

'Yeah, definitely,' I said but I was already blocking him from my profile.

I looked at the time on my iPhone. I'd just make the 16:41 at Finsbury Park and be home for dinner like I'd promised Mum. I dipped my head to check my face in his mirror, which was propped against the wall beside a collection of men's toiletries on the floor, and I zhoozhed up my hair.

He lay on the bed. I let myself out.

I slammed my Oyster card against the reader. I wasn't the first girl in year nine to have done it but I was the first in our group and it mattered. It was like winning a race. Having a big, vulgar, shiny sports cup on a mantelpiece that people would bend to look at and see themselves distorted by, and know that I was special. I stood on the tube, hovering, even though there were seats. I was scared I'd leave a stain. As the tube pulled out of Euston I felt him trickle out of me, mixed pink with my blood, warm and sticky, like melted ice cream.

Philippa Found has written three books about the body in women's art (FWSA prize nominated) and has short fiction published by Ether Books. She's completing her first novel, and a collection of darkly comic stories about female transformation – from an instruction manual on how to survive the art world to a sadistic makeover on a teenage girl.

MICHAEL GARVEY

Maggie

*An episode from a novel, as yet untitled, which weaves together the
lives of three people living in a small community in the west of Ireland.*

THE FAMILIAR CRUNCH OF GRAVEL OUTSIDE PROMPTED MAGGIE TO
grip the arms of her chair for support and rise to her feet. She hadn't
received post since the previous Monday, so Chris was sure to have
a bit of news for her, news of who had married, who had left, who had
come back, who was dying, but she knew she would miss him if she
didn't get the door opened in time. She never cared much for the post
he brought as she had long ago stopped receiving anything other than
electricity bills, election literature and booklets about referenda in
which she would not vote. Only at Christmas would she receive a card
from Eddie, but even that had been penned in someone else's hand for the
past few years.

She fumbled with the key, her jittery fingers struggling to turn it.
When she finally managed to open the door, cold afternoon light jostled
past her into the room. There was someone on the garden path, a rake of
a man with dirty blond hair and wide eyes: a stranger. He quickened his
pace as Maggie hastened to shut the door, but she was too slow. He held
the door open and leered in at her, his white van visible over his shoulder,
crouching by the roadside like a watchdog.

'How'ya?' he said. 'I'm with the Council.'

Maggie clutched the handle with one hand and worried at the hem of
her cardigan with the other.

'Only there were such bad storms back in February,' he continued, 'so
we're going around cutting down trees that might, eh, pose a threat.'

His accent wasn't local, but there were so many people who'd come
from elsewhere these days, people who'd married someone from the area

or found work in the town. And there was something familiar about his way of holding himself, his tousled hair, his smile.

'From the Council,' Maggie said. She had an eye on the sweeping bend of the road, but there wasn't a soul on it. 'Do you know Mike?'

'Ah, Mike, I do.' He smiled and she suddenly realised why he seemed familiar. He looked like her brother, his smile lighting up his face just as Eddie's used to. 'Big fella, isn't he?'

'He is,' Maggie said, her grip on the handle loosening.

'So listen, I'd say these trees could do with being cut,' he said, lifting his eyes to scale the evergreens that towered up next to her cottage. She remembered their terrible groaning on days when the wind howled in the chimney flue and buckets clattered across the backyard. The man looked young, hardly out of school, but it was good, she supposed, that the Council was taking on people like him. It might convince some of them to stay rather than jet off to Australia or America.

'I can cut them so they won't end up in on top of you, you know?'

He was nearly on the threshold. Perhaps he should be wearing a uniform with the Council logo on it – and didn't the Council vans that passed usually have writing on the side? But maybe it was his own van. There was no money for anything anymore, so it wouldn't surprise her if people had to use their own vans for Council work these days.

'Yes,' she said, for it would be a comfort to her to know that they wouldn't fall on the house during stormy weather, that she was safe.

'Great.' He was smiling at her now and he didn't seem so close, like he'd taken a step back. She knew she could be too wary of people sometimes, but she'd heard so many stories. 'I can get to work on them today then. Because they're not too far from the electricity lines and we wouldn't want them falling on those either, would we?'

'No,' Maggie said, her eyes flitting to the thin black wire drooping in the sky behind his head like a clothes line. 'What's your name?'

'Me own name's Jack, Jack O'Connor.' His smile spread the whole way across his face just as her brother's would. Eddie had always been the comedian in their house. It had been so long since she had seen him that it was his younger self she remembered best, how he had looked before he left, before he married, when their parents were alive and they were all still living under the one roof. She smiled.

'I have your approval to go ahead then?' he continued. 'Only, the Council is charging a small fee. You know how it is these days. Once

I have it I can get to work. I've the equipment in the back of the van.'

'How much?' Maggie asked. It was Wednesday, so she didn't have much of her pension left, but it'd be a shame not to get the trees sorted out while she had the chance.

'Just fifty euro. To cover the costs, you know?'

'Right,' Maggie said, a hand rising to her mouth as she tried to calculate how much she could scrape together. She cast him another glance. He was so like Eddie, smiling, slightly stooped, thick arms well used to lifting things. 'Can you wait a minute?'

'I can, yeah,' he said, shrugging as if he had all the time in the world.

It seemed rude to close the door, so Maggie left it open a crack. She went to the table and peered into the open mouth of her bag, then reached in and took out her purse. She found only a crinkled fiver and a handful of coins. Seven fifty in total. She clutched the note and the coins in her fist as she shuffled into her bedroom. The blankets were piled high on the bed and there was a lone cup and a scattering of scrunched-up tissues on her bedside locker. She knelt down before it and opened the top drawer, which contained a pool of receipts and Mass leaflets. She began to sift through them until her burrowing hand came into contact with the cold glass of a jar at the back of the drawer. She took it out with great care, as if the glass might shatter if she held it too tightly. Its label was green and faded and had upon it a garland of plump oranges surrounding an image of somebody's kitchen. The jar was lent weight by the coins that sat like sediment at the bottom.

She heard a sound, a quiet click, and her grasp on it tightened. She cocked her head and listened, but she heard only the keening of the wind. It had probably been a bird, its talons clicking on the windowsill or the roof. Or she might have imagined it. She was so sensitive to noise these days. The house had grown terribly quiet since her parents had died, so even the slightest creak startled her. It had never been a quiet house in her youth. There had always been the sputtering of the tap, the hum of the range, the staccato chopping of vegetables, the crackling music emitted by the wireless, the smack of Eddie's ball hitting the walls of the house, the grumble of the tractor and the sound of people talking, neighbours and family. But of course all that had stopped years ago.

When Maggie twisted the lid off the jar, she caught a whiff of bitter metal, the acrid tang of the coins trapped inside. She withdrew a crumpled roll of fives and tens. If she had seven fifty, she'd need forty-two fifty more. The speed with which she could do such calculations still filled her with pride. She had been praised for it when she had worked in the shop. She began to lay the notes on the bed, carefully flattening each with her hand. When she had laid out a ten and two fives, she heard a scuffing sound and shot a glance over her shoulder at the bedroom door, which she had left half open. Perhaps it had come from outside. Perhaps the man had grown tired of waiting and was walking around the garden. She returned her attention to the notes, but her hands were quivering and she worked quickly now.

When she had counted out thirty euro, the door's hinges squealed behind her and the sound was so familiar to her that she knew before she turned her head that he had entered, that he was in her bedroom, that he did not work for the Council. Her heart began to beat furiously. Suddenly he was at the bed, sweeping up the notes she had laid out. His eyes looked cold to her now, nothing like her brother's, and his smile had vanished.

'Ye never fuckin' learn, do ye?'

She tried to stem the flow of fear with silent pleas to God, but she could not focus on the words and her eyes kept darting back to him. He was rifling through her drawers, sending paper fluttering through the air. The last drawer contained her clean underwear, which he pulled out with his big, dirty hands, throwing them on the floor, emptying the drawer. She averted her gaze as the heat rose in her cheeks and she felt her eyes prickle.

'There has to be more,' he said. 'There's fuck all in this jar.' He shook it violently before her eyes, causing the coins within to chink loudly. 'I can waste my time looking, but you don't want that because time-wasting makes me very fuckin' angry.'

Maggie was still on her knees, which were beginning to cause her pain, but she couldn't move. Her heart was thumping so fast she was afraid it might give out.

'There's – there's no more,' she said.

'Don't fuckin' give me that! I told you I don't like time-wasting and you don't want to mess with me.'

'There's no—'

'No!' he shouted, his face a knot of anger, sharp lines shooting up between his eyebrows and around his mouth. He cast a glance at the window, then grabbed her by the shoulders, hunching down so his face was inches from hers, his eyes open wide, his breath thick and vinegary.

'If that's all the money, where's your jewellery? Necklaces, wedding rings and that. Where are they?' He shook her, his hands clasping her shoulders. 'Come on, woman!'

'They're – the box,' she said, her voice hardly more than a whisper. 'The dresser, on the dresser. But my mother – will you leave my mother's—'

He thrust her away from him, sending her sprawling. She felt her head hit the sharp edge of the locker, the blow translating into flashing white pain. Her teeth were knocked loose when her back hit the floor. She saw the pulsating white spot of pain gliding across the stippled ceiling and she heard a ringing sound, as if an alarm were going off in her head. She also heard the jangling of jewellery, the screeching of hinges, heavy footfalls and a crash, then the bark of an engine, the growl of the gravel. She tried to focus her mind on the words of a prayer, but her head was pounding and her leg throbbed insistently. She felt for something she could grab onto to lift herself up, but there was nothing. She could see the rippled surface of the radiator above her, the crawling foliage of the dark wallpaper, the white of the ceiling.

'Hello?' she called.

But the only sound now was the keening of the wind.

Michael Garvey is from County Kerry, Ireland. He graduated from Trinity College Dublin with a first class honours degree in French and English Literature. His writing has appeared in *Lighthouse, The South Circular, Visions: An Anthology of Emerging Kerry Writers, Wordlegs, The Irish Times* and elsewhere.

ALEX GOODWIN

Home Time

This is an edited extract from a (currently untitled) novel about three estranged siblings returning home in light of their mother's death.

THEY TOOK THE LIFT TO THE FOURTH FLOOR OF THE MULTI-STOREY car park, the one just by the Olympia exhibition centre, over the tracks from their mother's house. Experience had taught Lucille that the fourth floor was the only place you could be sure of finding a parking spot. For some reason the first three floors were always full, and she had long given up scouring the streets: most of the mansions in Olympia were empty investment eggs, and the same cars sat outside them day and night, never moving.

The fourth floor was a bittersweet place. Although it was damp and dark and the air was chock-full of exhaust, she used to love parking here – somehow it had become a symbol of her mid-twenties, the exciting days when she had just rented her first flat, started work at the practice, met Tyler: a time of energy, capacity, freedom. In those days, she felt thrilled she could just drive away afterwards, away from home and into her own life. The trouble started when she began wanting to escape her own life, the one she'd made, and didn't have anywhere else to go.

She told Joseph to wait by the entrance to the lift while she found the car. The darkness of the car park was comforting; no one could see her here. She passed rows and rows of cars, reached the end of a column and turned back. She had parked next to that purple Land Rover, hadn't she? No, must be a different purple Land Rover.

After ten minutes of searching she still couldn't find the car. She kept criss-crossing Joseph, who stood there like a pillar of jelly as she ran back and forth, her hands hurting from where her nails were pushing into her palms, until she stopped and checked the ticket in her purse. The ticket had the number five in the top right-hand corner, and she remembered she'd left the car on the fifth floor this time, because the fourth floor had been full.

They went up another level. She quickly located her car (next to another purple Land Rover) and buckled Joseph into the passenger's seat. She decided she would have to do something about his beard. It made him look like a wild man, a crank you might pass reciting the Book of Revelation outside a supermarket. She wondered if the razor she used for her legs would be enough to hack it off. Probably not. She should probably buy a new razor, trim the beard with scissors beforehand.

She wrinkled her nose and leant back; Joseph's sour smell was beginning to fill the car. He needed a bath and some clean clothes. She might still have some of Tyler's clothes somewhere at the back of the wardrobe; three years on and she kept finding odd things of his.

She gently touched Joseph's arm.

'Hey Joseph, hey. I'm sorry I couldn't come and get you earlier... I'm taking you back to my house, OK? Just for a while.'

He did not react. The emotional trauma had obviously produced some kind of shock, which was protecting him from realising what had happened. She would call Dr Herbert in the morning and make an appointment, ask for his recommendation.

She wound down the window to let in some stale car fumes.

'OK, right. Off we go, then. Home time.'

She turned the key in the ignition and they corkscrewed down the levels until they emerged onto the bright street. She turned left onto Hammersmith Road and headed east, cresting the bridge over the railway tracks. The traffic light was red; she stopped and felt disorientated, until she noticed the new glass-fronted apartment blocks on her right. The old Council offices must have been recently torn down.

The next turning on the left was Holland Road. A turn to the left and a turn to the right and she would be there. Her mother's house. The house that had belonged to her mother.

A car behind leant on its horn and Joseph started. The lights had turned green. Don't go, she told herself. You'll only upset yourself more. Go home, sort Joseph out, work out what you are going to do.

She lurched the car into gear and drove on, holding her breath until Hammersmith Road had merged into High Street Kensington and she was out into the long stretch of camping shops and perennially-closing suit outlets. The tall art deco monolith, once Barker's department store and now a Whole Foods, loomed at the end of the road, hinting at the point when she would be able to see the open green spaces of Hyde Park.

She exhaled. She had made the right decision. She didn't need any more drama. She was already weak with exhaustion and shock, and she was starving. Listen to yourself: you haven't eaten a thing all day. Be sensible. Get you and Joseph something to eat. Call William. Call Iona later, tonight, when the time difference is better; she's not a morning person, or at least, she wasn't. Run Joseph a bath. Run yourself a bath. When everything is taken care of, you can feel what you like.

She had tried to speak with her mother on the phone once a fortnight when visits to the fourth floor became scarcer and scarcer, after William, after the divorce, after her twenties car-crashed into her thirties, but it hadn't just been a lack of time that made visiting difficult. With all the junk and uncleanliness, the house had not been a go-to destination for an exhausted mother with a young child. There were always rusty nails on the floor, knives lying on tables, boxes of rubbish that might collapse on you at any moment – once she'd nearly been buried by a loose crate of empty picture frames.

The mess didn't seem to bother Joseph. He would often get agitated when she tried to clean the place up, like the mess was natural and not a sign of how the family had degraded over the past few years. This is not how it's supposed to be, she told him once. Don't you remember? It used to be clean, beautiful…

Her mother's birthday last September: Hestia had turned sixty-three. Lucille remembered that visit, parking on the fourth floor and insisting they all went out to breakfast at a local cafe before going for a walk around the Japanese garden in Holland Park. Hestia had insisted on wearing her large floral dressing gown, and Joseph had worn a crown made of tinfoil, which Hestia said he'd taken to wearing all the time recently, even in bed.

It had been an odd day. Joseph had been solemnly respectful to William, gravely offering him a slice of bacon at the cafe (which William duly received). She had no idea what was going on; they shared a secret language to which she was deaf. In the Japanese garden, Joseph had kept trying to spear the koi carp in the pond while Hestia covertly snipped the best roses off the bushes and hid them under her dressing gown.

William, encouraged, jumped into the zen sand garden and started digging a hole. They had been confronted by the park police and made to leave; Lucille had never felt so embarrassed.

Seven months ago.

That must have been the last time she went home.

She turned around.

Lucille left the radio on for Joseph and stepped out of the car, which she had left parked in a side street so he wouldn't be able to see the house. She shivered as she looked down the street: it was quiet and still. The house was the next-to-last one before the street met Holland Road; the last was a converted two-storey garage, the home of various businesses (none of which ever lasted longer than a year). A huge chestnut tree dominated the one end of the road, its branches still bare, balanced in the other direction by the vision of the arcing glass wall of the exhibition centre across the tracks, facing down the street like a setting moon.

All the houses on the street were the same style: three storeys, narrow, with black railings in front. Small rooms, intimate spaces. Lucille didn't know any of the neighbours; like the businesses, most of them moved in and out fairly rapidly, or left their houses vacant. It was an expensive neighbourhood, absorbed into the growing ghost town that was spreading out from Belgravia, Knightsbridge, Kensington; soon it would reach Hammersmith.

From the outside she noticed that the house had deteriorated quite badly since her last visit. Always the ugly sister on the street, it was now positively deformed. Paint flaked off the façade and large sections of rough masonry were visible around the darkened windows. A buddleia was growing out of the roof, just above her old bedroom window.

Lucille stopped before the door, then reached out and touched it. She remembered the door being bright green, with a brass knocker in the shape of a dolphin.

It had been smashed in. The central panel was splintered and pale, reinforced with steel plates driven into the wood with heavy bolts. The letterbox had been sealed up. She took Joseph's keys from her pocket, dropped them, but as she bent to pick them up she already knew that they wouldn't work. The lock was shiny, silver, evidently changed.

But the top of the door had remained relatively undamaged, and Lucille saw that someone had painted something in red paint. The paint was rough and thick – it must have been painted quickly. She was too close to read the words.

She stepped back: Do not trust the police.

She recognised the gesture behind them, the 't' and 'e' both executed with slashing horizontals, so characteristic of her mother's handwriting.

Alex Goodwin read English Literature at Bristol University, graduating with a First in 2007, before working as an assistant at Rogers, Coleridge and White, a literary agency in London. Last October he won the W&N/UEA Short Story Prize.

JOANNA GRAHAM

The Community

Chapter one of a novel.

G ALEN WORE A DOCTOR'S MASK AS EXTRA PROTECTION AGAINST HIS
allergies as he sat cross-legged in the grass under the open kitchen
window, eavesdropping on his parents' conversation. The clapboard
edges on the house's outer wall pressed into his back, but he stayed still.
His parents were discussing the best way to cook his grandmother's heart.

A bleached but sturdy wooden fence surrounded the green of his yard.
Beyond it, tall yellow grass grew around a slow stream in front of a birch
tree forest. If he took binoculars on clear days he could see deer grazing
between the trees. He'd found part of a carcass there last summer. The
doe's right front leg was missing, and the meat around her haunches had
been chewed away.

Galen knew his grandmother was dead. The phone had shocked
everyone awake at two in the morning to deliver the news. His parents
had hurried to the hospital and returned with a small blue and white
cooler just after the sun came up. He'd been following them ever since,
trying to overhear as much as he could.

Tomorrow there was going to be a burial, a eulogy and a wake. His
parents had explained their community's funeral customs at various
points when he was growing up, but this would be the first time he would
truly experience them, the first time he would be expected to consume
the deceased.

His grandfather had died ten years ago, but Galen hadn't been old
enough to eat solid foods then. His sister DD used to tell him he was
different from the rest of the family because he hadn't eaten the ceremonial
pie. His parents assured him they'd spoon-fed him some of the gravy.

'Do you think Robert will come?' Galen's mother's hesitant voice floated outside over the sound of onions frying on the stove. The sharp, sweet smell mixed with the cool smell of damp earth. His stomach growled; he hadn't eaten breakfast. His father didn't answer.

Galen had never met his Uncle Robert. He was the only person Galen knew of that had left the community. But before he'd left he was being raised to be the next community surgeon, the same position Galen was in now. His father always said Robert had abandoned them.

His mother continued. 'Lucy said she'd call him as soon as she got home.'

Galen's chest twinged. It would be strange for Aunt Lucy, coming home to an empty house. His eyes stung.

'I don't want him to,' his father said. 'I know he came for Dad's, but—'

'He should be with his family. Your mom would've wanted...' his mother trailed off. Tap water rushed into the sink, then stopped. 'Are you OK?' she asked.

'Right now, I'm just tired,' his father answered. 'We have to do this now?'

'Yes,' his mother said. 'It needs to cook as soon as possible, and slow cook. But I can take over from here. Go sleep.'

'No, I'll help you in here, then maybe we can both have a nap. I don't want to be alone today.'

The kitchen was quiet then, except for the sizzling. Galen rubbed his eyes, pushed himself up and walked to the back door. He took off his mask and shoved it in his jeans pocket as he stepped inside. The onions made his eyes water.

He wiped tears away and paused when he saw his parents. His mother was hugging his father and rubbing his back. His father was bent so his head rested on her chest, and his face was scrunched up, blotchy and wet. Galen's mother spotted Galen hovering and beckoned him to join them. As he did his father straightened, put one arm around him and one around his mother. Galen relaxed.

When they broke apart Galen poured a bowl of cereal and sat down at the kitchen table, watching his father peel rubbery bits of dead tissue from the brown lump on the counter. Galen stared, but couldn't reconcile the slab of muscle with the clean, precise diagrams he'd studied. His father sliced it in half and used the edge of his knife to prise wet, cobweb-like strings out of the deep red cavities inside. He cut the meat into cubes while Galen's mother moved the onions around with a long wooden spoon.

'He could still move back one day,' she said. 'You could talk to him about it.'

His father picked up the cutting board and slid the cubes into the onion pan. 'No,' he said.

'But he belongs here.' She checked the recipe beside her, focusing on the old piece of card paper until Galen's father replied.

'No he doesn't,' he said and put the cutting board and knife in the sink. 'I'm not going to waste my breath.'

Galen crunched his cereal and watched pink foam spread over his father's hands as he scrubbed the dishes. The smell of meat cooking made Galen's stomach rumble, even as he was eating.

The burial would be a quiet start to the ceremonial day, community members gathering to return his grandmother to the earth. Galen's family waited around the open grave while a dull grey sky hung over them, refusing to rain. Galen buttoned his suit jacket and crossed his arms. DD peered into the hole in the earth; her dark hair hung around her face so he couldn't see her expression.

His parents stood at the foot of the grave with fingers interlaced and arms folded together, leaning inwards so Galen couldn't tell who was supporting and who was leaning. His father wore a nicer suit than the ones he wore to work, and his dark hair was shinier and stiffer than usual. His mother wore a navy dress that matched his father's tie. Her dyed-black hair was swept into a low ponytail.

Aunt Lucy was between Galen and his parents in a long dress that trailed in the grass. She clasped her hands over her stomach and stared at the town. He followed her gaze towards Drummond.

It was a different perspective, but everything looked the same: one and two-storey buildings spread in a grid with the hospital looming above them from the centre of town. The haunted church was the second tallest building. Its high wooden spire looked white, even though Galen knew most of its paint had chipped off, making the structure seem diseased.

He heard engines and rolling tires before he saw four cars and a truck turn onto the cemetery's dirt road. The sound was comforting, but the quiet was even more present when the engines sputtered off and the guests stepped out. They were cousins, second cousins and however-many-times-removed cousins Galen saw regularly. They all clustered together before walking towards the fresh grave in an uneven line, the grass muffling their footsteps as they weaved between rows of tombstones. The group was smaller than he'd expected it to be; he hoped more people would come to the wake.

His parents and Aunt Lucy stepped forward to greet the approaching guests. They hugged and shook hands, exchanging whispered greetings and apologies. Their voices were more subdued than usual, not sharp enough to cut through the heavy air. They nodded at him and DD before settling into a semi-circle behind them.

Dinah, the community's current surgeon, arrived after the main group, hurrying through the graveyard to join everyone. She was a white-haired woman Galen knew well because of his regular visits to her office. She stood behind him and squeezed his shoulder. His throat tightened and he nodded instead of speaking, then looked into the grave beside his grandfather's. Beneath the brittle grass and pale, dry earth the base looked damp and grey. He expected something to move inside it – a worm or an insect – but nothing did. His grandparents' graves were at the edge of the graveyard. Behind them flat fields stretched to the horizon, interrupted by the low, scattered shapes of scarce and distant trees.

Three strangers appeared after Dinah: a tall man, a woman and a girl. The tall stranger was thin with glasses and a short beard. He looked familiar, but Galen didn't know why. He and his family stood apart on the opposite side of the grave. Galen could see the sky between their bodies.

None of them were still. The man was trying to keep his hands folded in front of him, but they kept straying to smooth his tie, adjust his pocket square or rub his chin. The woman was constantly shifting and Galen realized it was because her shoes were sinking into the earth and she had to keep readjusting her weight to pull them out. She was blonde, and something about her skin, her hair and the fabric of her clothes looked shiny and out of place. The girl was twisting and untwisting her long braid around her finger. She was blonde too, with a buttoned grey sweater that faded into the bleak sky. She looked bored.

Galen wanted them to go; they were intruding, but no one else was reacting to them. A few cousins glanced at Dinah and Galen's parents. His father's stare remained fixed on the grave, but Aunt Lucy's forehead tightened and the corners of her mouth twitched upwards; the tall man didn't return her smile.

Galen turned to DD, but four funeral attendants arrived with the coffin on their shoulders and he forgot what he was going to whisper to her. For several minutes Galen heard nothing but the wind and the deep, strained breathing of the mourners around him as they watched the coffin approach. He backed away as the attendants moved it over the grave, and, with a nod from his father, began to lower it.

Galen and DD moved closer to their parents. DD shivered against their father, who squeezed his arm tighter around their mother, who found Galen's hand and knit her fingers into his. The coffin hit the earth with a muffled thud. DD started to cry and Galen felt like the air had been pressed out of him. Two funeral attendants, a squat, middle-aged woman and a teenage boy, started shovelling dirt into the grave. Galen winced as it scattered over the coffin lid.

The tall man had wrapped his arms around himself. His chin was trembling, and he looked as if his body was about to collapse inwards. Galen decided it was OK for him to be there as long as he was upset. The man's family didn't comfort him. The girl fiddled with the hem of her sweater, and the woman kept her head bowed, looking at nothing but her own feet, until she touched his elbow and tilted her head towards the road. The three of them walked off, and Galen was relieved when they disappeared.

A few minutes later Dinah took her leave as well, patting Galen on the shoulder and nodding to his parents as she stepped away. The remaining guests followed her, touching his family in some way as they departed: a hand on his father's upper arm or a quick kiss on Aunt Lucy's cheek.

His immediate family lingered and watched the attendants fill in the grave. Galen thought about how the hole in the earth was being filled and wondered what had filled the hole in his grandmother's chest.

Joanna Graham is a Canadian writer from Winnipeg. She graduated from the University of Manitoba in 2012 with a degree in literature and was awarded one of the North American Bursaries from UEA. She is currently working on her first novel.

PAUL HOWARTH

Noone

*Extract from an early draft of a novel
set in Queensland, Australia, in 1877.*

M Y FIRST REAL EXPERIENCE OF THE WAR AGAINST THE BLACKS CAME
at age thirteen, when me and my brother Billy were out hunting
rabbits and strayed onto John Sullivan's land.

It was spring of seventy-seven and there'd been no rain for months.
We were up in the northern fields, combing the dusty scrub, rifles
slippery in our hands and our shirts soaked through with sweat. The
paddocks were barren. Grass as brittle as old bone and sharp against our
ankles, ochre soil fine as gunpowder underfoot. Father had shifted the
mob down-valley, closer to the creek; the only thing moving was the
flies. Every now and then the cicadas would start up, as if in retaliation,
showing the flies who was boss, and the air would be filled with their
rattling screams. Air so hot you could taste it. Singeing every breath.

'Should have gone down-valley,' Billy called. 'There ain't nothing up here.'

'It was you that wanted to come.'

'Only to keep clear of the mob. No other reason than that.'

We stood a moment, puffing slightly, swatting at the flies. I squinted
over the ruined paddock and uphill towards the stand of eucalypts
that marked the northern boundary of our run. 'Be cooler up there,' I
said, pointing.

'I ain't hot.'

'Me either. I'm talking about the rabbits.'

Billy considered it. 'Well,' he said finally, 'doesn't hurt to try.'

There was shade in the trees, sunlight dappling the deadfall and dry
leaves. I took off my hat and rubbed the sweat from my hair, sipped warm
water from my flask. I passed it over to Billy, he drank, then we parted

and began flushing between the blue-gums, no chance of silence, the deadfall crunching with each step.

Within fifty yards something bolted, crashing away through the brush, bigger than a rabbit judging by its sound. We gave chase. The heat suddenly forgotten, the thirst, the fatigue. Rifles in hand, we bounded over tree roots, weaved between trunks, racing each other as much as anything else. The pursuit didn't last long. With every stride it seemed the noise grew more faint, and soon both of us were slowing, following the trail at a jog, until Billy stopped and raised his rifle for a shot. It was pointless, the creature was gone, whatever it had been.

'I reckon a dingo,' Billy panted, lowering his rifle again.

'Too big, too noisy. It was probably just a roo.'

'Still, a roo's not bad. Hey – could have been a boar!'

I leaned against a nearby blue-gum and tilted back my head, imagining Father's face if we'd brought home a boar, the meal we would have had that night. I unstoppered my flask and took another drink. Ahead the trees were thinning, the beginnings of open ground. We'd almost cleared the forest: beyond lay Broken Ridge cattle station, John Sullivan's land.

'Come on,' I said to Billy. 'Let's go back.'

But my brother had noticed too, peering between the trees. He started walking and I followed, stepping hesitantly from the treeline like I worried the ground might give way. We weren't supposed to be up here. Father had once been Sullivan's stockman and though the pair still had some business together – Sullivan was our only neighbour for thirty miles – we'd been warned to keep our distance. Broken Ridge was out of bounds.

We stood looking over the sloping plains, at this corner of a kingdom a hundred times the size of our own. Sullivan's grandfather had settled the valley – in those days squatters took as much land as they could defend, no purchase, no lease. Our run seemed pitiful in comparison, nestled like an armpit alongside Broken Ridge, though at first the landscape didn't seem too different: bare scrubland pocked with buckbush and clutches of spinifex, termite mounds rising tall as a man. But in the distance I could see the feather-grass still growing, the basin of the valley improbably green, fed by the same river that flowed shin-high on our land. Far away on the horizon the jagged red ridge sawed at the sky, the foothills part-shadowed like they'd been wildfire-scorched.

'One man,' Billy said, staring. 'One man owns all of that.'

I shook my head. 'We should go.'

'We're not doing no harm.'

'But Daddy said not to – what if we're caught?'

'By who?' Billy said, laughing, opening his arms. 'Come on, don't be scared.' He slung his rifle on his shoulder and swaggered away.

'I ain't scared,' I called, trotting after him, picking my way through the rubble and cautious of snakes given the tracks smoothed into the dirt.

We'd gone less than a mile when I saw the horses coming over the rise, five hundred yards to the west. I grabbed Billy by the shoulder, pulled him down low. I counted nine riders in all, and behind the column of horses three men hobbled along on foot: blacks chained together by their necks. They were struggling to walk and when one stumbled the others did too, only to be hauled to their feet by the rear-most rider, jerking on the chain.

'Jesus, Billy,' I whispered. 'What're we going to do?'

'I don't know. Give me a minute to think.'

'Quickly or they'll see us.'

'All right – come on.'

Billy dragged me to a pair of Moses bushes growing thickly side by side. We crawled underneath, our shirts snagging on the prickles, then lay on our bellies and watched the procession, its progress soon halted when another of the chained men collapsed.

This one wouldn't get up. The rider snatched the chain but the man lay face down and didn't move. The rider dismounted. He was wearing a kind of police uniform: white trousers, blue tunic with a sash. He walked over to the man and kicked him. The body jerked and rolled. The other riders – some also in uniform – had turned their horses to watch. The police trooper was shouting. He slapped and hit the other two captives, bent low by the weight of the body on the floor. The trooper paused. He looked towards the front of the line, to a very tall man, not in uniform but well dressed in a tailcoat and city-style top hat.

The tall man nodded. The trooper shouldered his rifle, stood over the fallen prisoner, pointed, and fired. The body flinched. The shot tumbled across the plains. Billy and me looked at each other. Neither of us spoke. There was panic in my brother's eyes and I could feel my heart beating against the ground. The riders cheered and clapped. The chained blacks cowered. The trooper knelt to unlock the body from the neck-cuff, then shook out the chain and pulled the others upright. He remounted.

Leaving the body in the dirt, the party rode on a short distance, before all but the last horse broke into a gallop, veered around, and came thundering directly towards where me and my brother hid.

Billy let out a moan like a kicked dog.

'Let's run for it,' I whispered. 'Beat them to the trees.'

'We never would, Tommy. We both have rifles – they'll shoot us in the back.'

'So what'll we do? Billy, what'll we do?'

He crawled out of the bushes and climbed to his feet, eyes pinned on the riders now only a hundred yards away. With his rifle in the air he edged into open ground, shouting, 'Don't shoot! Don't shoot!' as the riders drew up before him in a line. He was trembling, his legs jagging back and forth at the knees, staring at the men who were unlike any police I had ever seen. Five uniformed natives, all of them armed, two with their rifles aimed directly at Billy's chest.

The other three men were white: John Sullivan; his offsider, Locke; then the tall man in the hat, who I didn't know. He was lean as a cat and wore a finely-patterned waistcoat and high leather boots. His moustache was thick and neatly groomed. Sitting erect in the saddle, he kept back from the rest of the group and began with the makings of a pipe.

'You would be Ned McBride's boy, I take it?' Sullivan said. The squatter was short and plump, his filthy shirt looking fit to burst.

'Yessir. Billy McBride.'

'And the other one?'

I felt my innards quicken. 'Get out here,' Billy hissed. 'Tommy, come on.'

I edged out of the cover and went and stood so close to my brother I could feel his fingers brushing mine. I was shaking. Eyes downturned, I saw flecks of dried blood on the shins of Sullivan's horse.

'And you?' Sullivan asked me.

'This is my little brother, Tommy.'

'He don't speak for himself?'

Billy elbowed me. I looked up. 'Yessir. Tommy McBride.'

'Good,' Sullivan said, smiling. His hair was wild, his face unshaven, his cheeks mottled as if by drink. 'Well, I'm guessing you know who I am, so perhaps you can tell me what you're doing with those rifles on my land.'

'We didn't mean nothing by it,' Billy blurted. 'We was hunting rabbits in the trees and got lost.'

'Didn't notice the clearing when you crossed it?'

'We thought we'd found a dingo so kept going, that's all.'

'A dingo?' Sullivan said. He glanced at Locke and smiled. 'Well, there's plenty of them about, but past them trees they're mine to shoot, not yours.'

'Ain't they but everyone's?' Billy asked quietly. 'Since they're wild?'

'Sounds just like a nigger,' Locke said. Hunched forward in the saddle, he glanced back towards the chained blacks, and spat.

'No, they ain't *but everyone's*,' Sullivan said. 'Everything on my land belongs to me, same as the cattle. Unless that's what you really came for, hmm?'

'We was hunting, not duffing,' Billy answered. 'Them's two different things.'

Sullivan stared at him, let the silence hang. 'You're probably wondering about my associates here. Well, the man at the back is Sub-Inspector Edmund T Noone of the Native Mounted Police. These are his troopers, and their business is the dispersal of those who don't belong here. Chiefly that means niggers, but Mr Noone's skills aren't particular to the colour of a man's skin... boys, he knew you were hiding in those bushes probably before you even got there yourselves.'

I glanced at Noone then quickly away. Thick pipe smoke dribbled from his mouth and drifted over his face like a caul.

'Now usually,' Sullivan continued, 'Mr Noone likes to punish trespassers to the fullest extent of the law. To disperse them, as it were. But since this is my land, I suppose I have a say, so I'll agree to let you go on two conditions: first, that I never find you hunting up here again...'

He paused and looked at Billy, who nodded eagerly in reply.

'And second, that you be sure to tell your father exactly what happened here today, understood?'

'Yessir,' Billy said eagerly. 'Yessir, we will.'

'And you?'

Again Billy elbowed me. I looked up at Sullivan and nodded.

'To my thinking a deal should be agreed out loud.'

'Say it, Tommy.'

I swallowed. 'Yessir.'

'Good,' Sullivan said, taking up his reins. 'Then on your way.'

All of them left save Noone. Sitting motionless in the saddle, smoking his pipe, he watched us with eyes that were small and very white. The gaze felt hot and sharp and I could not return it, though I had the sense that Billy alongside me was trying his best. Noone had his head tilted, studying us like lame calves he was deciding whether to put down.

I took hold of Billy's arm and pulled him away, hurrying for the trees and the safety of our land. The first three times I glanced back over my shoulder Noone was still sitting there, watching us. The fourth time I looked he was gone.

Paul Howarth is a British-Australian former lawyer now living in Norwich and writing his novel *Noone,* a historial thriller set in the late nineteenth century on the Queensland frontier. At UEA he is the recipient of a Malcolm Bradbury Memorial Bursary.

COLLEEN HUBBARD

The Flack

WHEN THE PIX CAME OUT, MY COMPANY WENT INTO CRISIS MODE.
That was my occupation – crisis PR – but the Boss got a special thrill
by sending messages with the subject line CRISIS MODE before 4 am.

I flipped open my laptop to assess the situation. Nudie pix. OK, right,
we just needed to launch Strategy MBWA, which usually worked well.
And of course we had to get clients to sign up for the comprehensive suite:
monitoring every channel, posting comments, ensuring the right sort of
paparazzi coverage. $20,000 a month, a small investment, really.

'My Boyfriend Was Away,' the actress said tearfully.

If I was stuck filming in Burbank and my boyfriend was in Australia, I'd sure
as hell send naked selfies – commenter 4719 (actually, me)

Actress and boyfriend photographed holding hands in a bodega as they
scope out juice options. (Note that actress is a paid representative of
N'Orange, the zero calorie orange drink).

But this time, this crisis mode, was different. It was a huge dump of
photos, several actresses, more leaking by the hour. A couple of our girls
were in there, nothing too difficult. But then there was Sukia.

'Little asshole,' Boss said when I got into the office.

I didn't take it personally. Little asshole was just our pet name for Sukia.

You know her, or your kids do. She was huge on that show with kids
who met in a treehouse every afternoon, except it started getting weird

when they filmed too many seasons and had to raise the roof of the treehouse to accommodate the boys' height.

Sukia was the star. Half-Russian ('The other half pure asshole' – Boss), she looked like a doll with big lashy eyes that might blink if you tilted her. We repped her through her first crisis, when she left the show before her contract ended and the producers leaked how terribly she'd treated people on set.

> *i wouldn't stay on that dumb kids show i mean those other*
> *kids are just kinda community theatre rejects amirite?*
> – commenter bowwowbao (me)

Sukia visiting a children's hospital, handing out Treehouse Gang dolls to patients. (In the limo on the way over, she borrowed a ballpoint pen and quietly stabbed the eyes of her rival's doll).

There's something I should say at this point, because it figures into the rest of the story.

I'm not sexually interested.

I don't mean in Sukia – I mean, of course, I'm not interested in Sukia – I'm not interested in anyone. It happened maybe five years ago. I had been a perfectly normal guy – porn, scoping out prospects at the gym – but then I couldn't make it happen. I looked at this guy who had picked me up at a PR event, someone who was exactly my type, and when he took off all his clothes I thought nah. Wanna see what's on TV? And my interest never came back.

Why I'm telling you this is because my total lack of sexual interest made me the ideal candidate for what came next. That whole nest of pictures – I had to look through it. Sukia, little asshole, supreme teenage fuck-up, in stills and video. No MBWA option on this one, because she wasn't alone in the pix.

'A three-way with chicks we could manage,' Boss said. Boss was 55, though she claimed to be 42. She kept her silver hair in a hard bob, which looked like a helmet and gave her the air of a retired general in the sex wars. She leaned into the screen to decode the tangle of limbs and implements. 'I don't even know what's happening here. Is that a weather instrument? You know, for three thousand years people fuck like cavemen, and all of a sudden these kids need to invent new shit?'

I coughed and then excused myself to get a mug of green tea.

Later, looking through the pix, I saw something else. This woman with strawberry-blonde hair. Images that looked a little older than the rest. Not vintage, just not exactly contemporary. Because of my sex thing, or my not-sex thing, I have this particular insight you might not expect. I know what sexy is.

I know this sounds ridiculous, but hear me out. Everyone else has taste. Studio heads, casting directors, agents, scouts, the bartender. They look at a girl or a guy and they think, 'Yeah, I would.' They don't think that because they have some kind of calculator to work out mass appeal; they think that because of personal taste.

I don't have an appetite. None. So when I look at a photo, I don't think, 'Wavy black hair, like I like.' I just think: yes. Or: no. Mostly no.

Strawberry blonde was a yes. A big yes. I couldn't figure out why, and I didn't need to, either. The other weird thing was that I couldn't place her. The other pix in the leak, maybe 400, were all recognizable stars. That girl from that talking cat show, the hot weather guy who went viral with a supercut of him saying 'blowy' over and over.

Strawberry blonde I knew from nowhere. I searched the message board where the leak was released to see if anyone had ID'd her. No dice. I sent a couple links to Boss w/r/t Sukia, just comments she should be aware of in case her blood pressure spike had started to decrease. The thing about Boss is that she's actually happier when she's full-steam insane.

Then I went home, dropped a flowering tea ball into a goblet of boiling water, and watched it unfurl, each petal leaning back in a slow yawn. The doorbell rang. I let Jamie up.

I'd heard of this service a year ago and so far liked it. I'd describe it as somewhere between prostitute and personal assistant. Jamie didn't have sex with me (although he would for the right price, I guess) or do my laundry (again, who knows?), he just sort of hung out and I paid him. Also he was hot and I could bring him to parties.

He also liked, or pretended to like, the nature shows I enjoyed, the ones where it's a family of hedgehogs and the camera somehow follows them for the whole season: birth, winter, the death of Grandpa Hedgehog, spring.

'Did you see there's a new one about lorikeets?' Jamie said, pouring himself a drink.

I was still on the couch looking at my flower bomb, now completely deployed, though I hadn't taken a sip. The water had gone cool.

'Rough day?' Jamie asked.

I slid my laptop toward him and showed him the pix.

'Right,' he said as I scrolled. 'I saw that.'

I paused at the picture of the strawberry blonde.

'Radhia,' he said.

'What?'

Jamie took a big gulp of wine. He could drink too much now because he was young, but he wouldn't always be.

'Radhia,' he said. 'My dad had a picture of her in the garage above his workbench. Pretty sure she's from that country where everyone died.'

I sipped cold tea and looked her up. PR isn't about endings, is the thing. PR believes in the new beginning, the chance. The next big step. Mars, Jupiter, beyond. Stupid non-planet Pluto, then whatever is after Pluto that we'll discover and then demote. That's what Boss would say, but the reality is that we're self-centered. When there's a real crisis, like when all of those people on Radhia's island were killed, there were memorials for weeks. I remember someone in the office wearing a ribbon. Or maybe that was just fashion. But then we moved on.

'So she's dead then,' I said, looking at her skimpy Wikipedia entry, which showed her place of birth and an estimated death date in brackets.

'I guess,' Jamie said. 'If not dead, at least old. Late 30s or early 40s? For your purposes, dead either way.'

I should pretend to be embarrassed that I immediately started plotting. I'm not good with shame though, never was. After Jamie ordered dim sum, we settled onto the couch for 'Lorikeets: Heaven in the Clouds,' but my mind was ticking.

If I didn't recognize her, most people wouldn't. Here was a tragic star. She was beautiful and dead. If I could find a way to make her a thing, something that could make me a few bucks, I could also get out of crisis PR. My mortgage was paid off, I had cash in the bank, and I just needed something to keep my interest so I didn't turn into a golf robot.

So that's how I got to where I am now. I contacted a few archivists to help me find images and videos. Not just more: I wanted all of them. I hoarded a stockpile and hired specialists to create a brand as well as some custom images. They made edits to some pix I owned, popping Radhia's head on models' bodies, so that I'd have pix that weren't available elsewhere because they didn't exist. I bought rights to her old films, cheap monster movies that were made in her home country.

OMG that girl? I was OBSESSED with her.
Whatever happened to her?

– commenter alfonseG on news of her films being screened in
Chinatown as a double feature (and this actually was not me)

The thing I know, after years of this, is that you want it because you can't have it. That's why Sukia's crisis was a crisis. Because if you thought that she was indiscriminating, then you couldn't fantasize that you were special. It was your sense of humor, your charm, that sparkle in your eye. That's awful, you say, but it's true. That's why a dead bombshell is the best bombshell: Diana, Brigitte, Verity, Cerrada, and now Radhia. No one can have them, not even you, but in that way, they are yours completely.

Recently Jamie dropped by. I hadn't seen him in a couple weeks. He asked to borrow a couple thousand, to tide him over until the check arrived from some catering job.

I was looking through the cabinets when he asked, sure that I had disposable chopsticks somewhere.

'I'm sorry to ask,' Jamie said. 'It's just that I don't think I can make rent.'

I closed the cabinet and turned to him. He was thinner than the last time I'd seen him, but his face looked like he hadn't slept in weeks. I said we'd figure it out.

We got onto the couch and I pulled a blanket over us. It was a surprisingly chilly night. I gave a voice-command to the screen, which flicked on, and then we scrolled through the available programs. One of Radhia's movies was airing.

'Ch-ching,' Jamie said.

He was right – I'd get a little something, but not much.

The monster was cheap looking, made of common household goods. Her country's film studios never had money, and the budget was invested in buckets of fake blood. Jamie's eyes closed, which gave me the chance to look at him without him flexing or posing. I decided then that I'd take care of him, or try, at least.

Though he fell asleep, I kept watching. I'd seen this one, of course, but that didn't lessen the appeal. This was Radhia's first movie. She was just a girl then, maybe 16, and you can see the inexperience when she's hanging at the edge of the screen, not sure what to do. She looks a little lonely. At one point, she sticks her hands in her pockets, although she's with a pack of students supposedly being terrorized by a demon beast that invades high schools.

Finally, her big moment. She wasn't the main actress, and because of this, she couldn't survive.

Her death came in a dark forest. The camera took the monster's POV as it chased her, following her long red hair like a lit match flickering through the dark. Radhia stumbled. Radhia fell. She tried to get up, but fell again. She turned around and looked at us. Her eyes said please no. But we were the monster, and we were upon her.

Colleen Hubbard is an American writer living in London.

CAITLIN INGHAM

Blue

The beginning of a short story.

A BAR, LATE AT NIGHT, IN THE DEPTHS OF WINTER. ALL BITING dreariness, all new vows smudged and turned bitter. Peasants, Producers, Queens, Barons, Bankers, Witches and Bitches, we sucked on rhubarb pickle sours and tipped Earl Grey whisky martinis into our gullets. Snorted up fairy powder and blew out smoke from the damp arse-end of buildings. Clinging to the dregs of festivity to make it through the first month of the unwelcome fresh year.

It's a strange sort of girl who fears ending up alone, when they have a phone frothing with dates and the puny, pale beauty of a thirteen-year-old Russian supermodel.

I was she.

But although it was a fragile and tedious time, I had never gone as far as to talk to *him*. Not the blue-bearded prick who sat at the corner table!

He liked being called 'Blue' and would sliver into the place without anyone noticing, making you feel like he was everywhere. Before too long your eyes would be involuntarily pulled towards his cement smile or you'd overhear one of the compliments that leaked from his mouth like bad breath.

Admittedly, I'd had one brief encounter with him, when I'd been trying to walk to the little girls' room three months prior. He had been dating a haggish ex-ballerina at the time and they had been high as treehouses and pulled me into their little scrum, squishing a glass of champagne into my hand. In return, I'd sloshed the bubbles onto the woman's dress and then squeezed out a putrid, tumultuous fart right onto the blue-bearded prick's lap.

He'd left me alone since then, but I'd seen a flicker of admiration on his fat face.

That night he was sat at the bar, alone for once, stroking the hairs on his chin, which must have been bleached and then streaked with the pretentious periwinkle. I felt his eyes crawl over me like slugs. I tried to trawl through my messages to select a suitor, but Salvo the barman interrupted.

'Blue *cannot* stop staring at you tonight.'

'I know, how disgusting.'

'He's just broken up with his girlfriend… you should go for it!'

'Why on earth would I do that? He is repulsive.'

'Wait, sweetheart. You don't know?'

Salvo stopped still but his hair quivered like a chihuahua.

'He's a celebrity. He's BFFs with Taylor Swift and has Instagram followers all over the kingdom.'

I gripped my taut thighs with confusion. 'What? Well how come I don't recognise him?'

'Oh you know, he keeps it real. But I swear, when he's not here he's like, reading out poems with James Franco or blowing out birthday candles with Blue Ivy. And he doesn't even drink now but still tips like Richie Rich with a hard-on.'

I inspected my friend's face and saw it was earnest and true.

I looked over at the blue beardy prick. His oily, milky cheeks reflected the flashing lights of the dance floor quite sweetly. On second thought, the beard, perhaps, was not periwinkle, but electric blue instead. Bowie had electric blue hair at one point. Did he not write a song about it? Maybe it was actually an excellent look and I just hadn't got it. I flushed with embarrassment at the thought of his sophistication fooling me; what a naive little chicken I could be. An unwelcome memory of my chubby eleven-year-old-self eating liver and onion pie with my moustachioed grandma popped into my mind. I clenched my fist and banished it.

He saw me looking and raised his enormous pink milkshake. Jabs of jealous maiden scowls prickled around the room. Salvo winked and cackled as I strode over; the evening was sparking up. Blue licked his chops and rubbed his thick knees when I sat down with him. I allowed my mink to slip slightly and expose a hint of my white breast.

'Madame,' he kissed my hand with damp fish lips, 'so psyched you finally came over.'

'Darling, I feel as if I were made of stone until this second.'

We spoke a little of our dreams and desires, our beliefs and aspirations. At one point we got Salvo to take a picture of the two of us and Blue uploaded it and said: *Who says you can't find beauty in Brooklyn? #bae #thisgirl #Tuesday #drinks #princess*

Kanye West 'liked' it.

By spring I had turned into a kept woman. I swapped boozing for volunteering and took up teaching scat singing to a group of old blind people. My plump little prince kept me happy. I even dyed a tuft of my pubic hair blue as a tribute to him!

I gauged snippets of the origins of his great fortune. He was one of the early app and website creators for Elderly Elixir, which rejuvenated the faces and phrases of selected over-fifties and disposed of those too decrepit to hope. And then there was his zine – *Superior Stepmothers* – that championed the plight of second wives that deserved more attention than their new hubby's children.

His schedule was sporadic. Sometimes we would snooze and laze around the apartment for days on end, waited on by his excellent selection of servants. We'd nibble sushi, master dance routines, he'd make me squeal with laughter with his imitation of a disabled duckling. Other times, I would barely see him for a week. I would potter about, whiling away the moments, singing my *oodleh aw wap doo dah*. The staff would watch with pained, solemn expressions, obviously deeply moved by my new talent.

Blue would always manage to catch me off guard on his return. I'd inevitably be doing something vaguely mortifying, like flicking through one of his ex-wives' modelling portfolios or eating half a slice of bread like a little piggy. Then I'd hear, 'My little ladylove!' or 'My precious poo petal' and I'd whip around and see that creamy smile and blue, heart-shaped spurt of facial hair.

The only thing I couldn't get him to relent on, however much I wriggled and jiggled, was the secrecy surrounding his so-called *studio space*.

'It's private, baby,' he'd say, 'it's my sacred abode. Victoria and David were actually just saying last night how much of their relationship was based on trust and respecting boundaries.'

But the studio was out in the bugger-up end of Queens, so of course, I knew he was hiding something – or someone. A mistress perhaps? That seemed nigh impossible given how devoted he was to me. Perhaps it was a drug ring of some sort? A cupboard stuffed with dwarves dallying out powder into little sacks? But then my darling had been to rehab and never touched any of the naughty stuff, so that seemed doubtful. I couldn't imagine. But I had to find out.

Of course, the second I actually wanted my husband to leave, the longer he seemed to hang around. There was just one engagement after the other. Flings and swing dancing ping-pong comps. Bear fights, cock duels, rock lights, diamond fuels. I was supple on my husband's arm and would twiddle a strand of his tuft so people passing would be mildly blinded by my jewelled fingers. He was very proud, but I knew he'd had a checkered list of brides before myself, and it was getting harder and harder to stick out from the pack. One thing that aided me was my siblings. Blue flew them first-class from their various pecking patches around the globe and scrubbed them all clean in a spa until they were almost as attractive as me. The three of us exuded nymph-like naivety whilst flashing our foxy little fangs, and had most of the crowd salivating.

But after a while, all this began to wear thin and my thoughts were pulled again and again to his studio. I wanted to truly know the man I had married. I wanted to delve into my husband's psyche and attempt to understand what went on behind the flaccid white of his eyes.

It was no joke getting Driver to agree to take me to the studio. Clearly it was seriously forbidden. I resorted to sneaking a whole manner of crushed pills into his apple smoothie every morning until he was drowsy, constipated and psychotic in equal measures. Then I pinned him down and got one of the worse singers in my group to scat in his ear until he screamed he would do anything to make it stop. We set off the very next day. My heart thumped under my tiny bosom and my hands grew sticky on the leather as the postcard skyline morphed into unknown scabby tower blocks.

'One mustn't stray off the path around here, I suspect?' I called out to Driver. 'All wild dogs and hungry smackheads?'

He did not respond. Lord, was I nervous! We drove past dirty, looming buildings with mismatched bricks, swarming pigeons and creeping tramps. Hounds pattered by without leashes or humans to hold them, seemingly unabashed by their wildness. Grim-faced cops, mucky teens charged the pavements whilst howling toddlers declared war from prams.

What could possibly make Blue subject himself to this dreary and disgusting patch of the city? The more vile the neighbourhood became, the more I wanted to know what was in that sodding studio. Driver's thick hairy fingers gripped on to the steering wheel as the car started to slow.

'My, oh my,' I leaned forward, 'what mighty hands you have!'

'What? Oh yes, my ex-wife used to make me wax them. Now, here we are. I'll wait outside here in the car until midnight. Building code is seven-three-seven. You have to follow the sign for the bagel stand, the studio is just on top of that.'

'Oh, do come in with me darling,' I said. 'Don't be such a bore.'

'No madam. I think you'll find that I have held up my end of the bargain. I won't go any further.'

'Oh fine then, you wet pair of panties, I'll go in alone.'

Before I got out of the car I doused my finger in my saliva and then jammed it into his earhole to demonstrate my disappointment. He accepted my punishment in silence.

The building was painted lime green with bubblegum borders around the windows and doors. Billboards for peanut butter cookie bars and cinnamon chili popping corn were emblazoned on the front. 'Oh, my beardy poppet,' I muttered stoically as I jabbed in the entrance door code. 'What are you hiding from me? What would make you come to such a frightful place?'

Inside was as endless as a public hospital, looming grey corridors shooting off from every direction, mountains of junk in the corners and rats relaxing on the stairs. I barely had to follow the signs for the bagel stall, as the slobbish inhabitants or workers had left little carby crumbs all over the floor. I knew I had reached my husband's studio from the blue paint and the diamond-encrusted frame, so at odds with the rest of the grimy hallway. I looked down at my fingers and saw I was shaking. I realised for the first time I was frightened of what I was about to do, of my disobedience, my quashing of our love and our routine.

Was it wrong that I wanted to uncover my husband's secret? Did I really know him at all? I considered turning back. Perhaps I could bribe Driver to help me douse the building in petrol and flick an impish match on the whole structure and its unsavoury inhabitants.

But I guess I'm but a simple gal, and I wanted to understand the man I had married. I breathed deep, gripped on to the handle and let myself into the room.

Caitlin Ingham was born in 1990 in London and grew up mostly in Yorkshire. She studied English Literature at Queen Mary, University of London and then spent two and a half years at David Godwin Associates as an assistant literary agent before coming to UEA.

MALACHI MCINTOSH

Touch

Chapter one of a novel.

BOOM. THE CRASH RATTLES THE HOUSE, KNOCKS FLAT ALL THE ornaments on her television set, ripples through the carpet, shifts the curtains, makes even the air, for a moment, fizz. Her first thought is blank; before she realizes what's happening she's up at her window, cranking flat her blinds to stare across her sunburnt front lawn and picket fence to a single car on its back and burning black smoke. The road both ways is as vacant as always – just an infinite strip of asphalt headed west one way and east the other, desert all around and nothing to make you slip or skid, but still, somehow, a flipped-over car breathing fire.

She's thinking now and talking to herself. She knows for miles and miles around there's nobody, says it out loud, 'Nobody', breathes in air and watches the wreck, then decides.

'OK,' she says and starts moving, pulling her hair back. 'All right Mary. OK. Let's go.'

Jake, her dog – so rheumatic, deaf and half-blind that the fast crack boom caused by the car's somersault only made him raise the wisps of his eyebrows – just barely lifts his head as she scrambles around, then he sets it back down.

She searches first under her couch, sliding her forearms into the tumbleweeds of fluff and dirt, then dashes up into her kitchen onto cold tile, its chill on bare feet making a weird contrast with the fire she still sees streaming up from the car in the street. Her bedroom next, closet, a pile of laundry she needs to do, a single flipflop and more dust, boxes of old unworn high heels. Fuck it, she thinks, still looking, and then she's running barefoot to the threshold, slow down the handful of steps into her scrubland lawn, across the yards of it, the car like an apocalypse in front of her and somehow – as she thought – no bodies near it, just all that fire. It takes her longer to get out there than she wants it to, her knees and hip pain getting worse every day, but then she's there, just a few feet away, and stops.

She doesn't know anything about new cars. The body – one of those smooth plastic bodies – is on its head, half on and half off the road, smoke and fire raging from some space between the front tires and out around an axle, below all that somebody's white arm, palm up and blood on it, fingers extending with screams she hadn't heard before but hears now as if she's screaming herself.

She feels paralyzed, feels her own pulse, the air like a mouthful of burnt matches, a throatful of exhaust. She crouches down without thinking, coughs, her chest in search of better air, eyes at the billowing smoke, the broken car; eyes at the arm – lower to the ground, a better view: there's a little boy trapped upside down and limp in the back, doll-like in a car seat, his mom up front – the one reaching her broken arm – and something like a man slumped forward and – it's hard to tell – all that smoke – all this endless smoke like hellfire all around them. Is there even a man? 'Are you all right!?' she yells, but of course no one says anything and they're not. If everyone isn't knocked out yet they almost are – the car upside down, on fire, and possibly about to explode. 'I'm gonna… I'm gonna try to get you all out!' she yells, but the words make it worse; she still can't move, still doesn't know where to start, the hand out the window still grasping for something it can't quite touch. 'My name's Mary,' she says, just to say something else. She gets flat on her stomach under the smoke, although there really is no underneath it now. 'I'm Mary,' she says. 'I don't know what I'm doing.' All the windows are open, at least. 'I'm gonna get you all out of here. I'm gonna get you all out and call some help for you. You're all gonna be fine. I'm gonna get you all out, all of you, and you're all gonna be fine. So just wait a second.'

During all the talk she drags herself forward on her stomach, chin just above the dirt, and slides her arms into the car and starts to unbuckle the child, a little girl not a little boy, maybe Indian – it's so hard to see and breathe – a tangle of arms and legs, dark hair, definitely, long dark hair, beautiful like a princess's even in all this and she has her now, she has her out, and slides back, inches back out of the car like a worm in the dirt, crawling backwards, contracting her body, crawling back and back and back until they're out, just beyond and she runs.

A beautiful, pristine little girl, maybe five or six years old in her arms, and she's running. She takes the girl a hundred feet or more away from the car and steels herself, two more trips in and out she thinks, and then the car explodes.

Not a series of perfect spheres expanding outward in overlapping, exotic color: just a loud noise, sharper than the earlier crack boom and pieces flying and flame and even more fire. The weight of the air knocking her straight back into the grass.

Caught in her arms, the little girl, coughing.

But Mary isn't thinking anymore. The body of the car is burning, more or less on her front step, no one anywhere near her and this little girl is coughing and her eyes – she has dark eyes – and Mary's heart is wild and the hand out the front window opening and closing and then the explosion. She leaves the girl, eases her onto the ground, gets up, tender, and runs at the car but can't get near it because of the heat, the intense heat worse than anything she's ever felt. Her body steps her back and back and then the little girl is crying behind her and babbling and Jake comes forward, from somewhere, slowly, and barks an old man's bark that tires him out and makes him slump down and her mouth is so dry and she has no breath, and then, backing away from it, the hellfire, toward her house, to dial 911, her chest clenches, her legs go limp, and she goes down.

Malachi McIntosh was born in Birmingham, England and raised in the United States. He writes fiction and criticism and has had work published in *Fugue, Broadcast, Under the Radar, The Guardian, Wasafiri, The Journal of Romance Studies, The Caribbean Review of Books* and *Flash.* The extract above is from a novel-in-progress titled *Fame.*

EMMA VICTORIA MILLER

The Covenant of Blood

This is a section of a gothic novel that features two intertwined
narratives: a contemporary narrative set in the South of England,
and a nineteenth-century narrative set in North Yorkshire.
Both are stories of greed, ambition and incest.

DEMI-PLIÉ IN FIRST, SPINES PULLED STRAIGHT, AN AVENUE OF legs concertina into a grand-plié, right arms all extended in unison. Twenty different heads follow the curve of each taut sunlit limb, fingers delicately grouped, index fingers and thumbs reaching to complete the movement into second position, before drawing the arm smoothly through the preparatory position and starting again. Twenty girls, moving together like graceful marionettes, their beauty belying their strength. An unlikely army preparing for an as yet unimaginable battle. Bodies that are riddled with rebellious hormones, which strain against dictates in every other aspect of their lives, are here compliant to the commands of their unlikely drill sergeant, Ria Waters. I try and absorb their self-control by concentrating on the execution of their movements, my muscle memory twitching to perform the well-remembered routines, as my disobedient mind imagines an alternative Saturday – one where I stayed at home.

'We don't often see you here.' Aurelie's cut-glass accent slices through the daydream with all the destructive force of a Hitchcock killer.

'I just thought I'd check in and see how she's getting on,' I reply, turning away from the large window that overlooks the studio and trying to think where to put myself.

It is an oddly charged environment, the peripheries of a dance class, with its cliques of mothers, helpers and hangers-on, all crushed together on the viewing platform. Elevated above the washed-out YMCA décor of the foyer, we observe the girls perform as if they are a dangerous species better contained behind safety glass. I'm no good in the audience – when I'm nervous I prefer to move. But movement is not an option on this side of the glass, and so I must stand or sit, my life a performance of *Coppélia* in reverse, from animate girl, charming an audience with the fluency of her movements, to inanimate doll, grotesque and immobile as a corpse.

The usual suspects are crowded in a semi-circle on the small viewing platform, six fully grown women with party plates on their knees in readiness of the M&S picnic brought by the pack leader, Aurelie Martin, a woman who already has one boy at Elmhurst and who'll be damned if her youngest girl doesn't follow suit, despite Lexie's flat feet and fast expanding glamour model proportions. Aurelie herself is of the hunting, fishing, town house in St John's Wood, country pile in the Home Counties sort of upper-class Londoner, built like a brick wall but strangely obsessed with defying both nature and nurture to turn her children into dancers, controlling and containing their every movement like dolls in a music box.

'Well, I have to say,' Aurelie adds after a protracted pause, 'from what I've seen, Cassandra hardly ever puts a foot wrong, but then I suppose with your family's pedigree we wouldn't expect anything less.' The words are delivered without malice, but with a kind of absent-minded resentment as she watches Lexie's laboured battements.

'She works hard,' I answer, a little testily, as the other mothers turn from their gossiping to see if there will be a confrontation; it wouldn't be the first time, some of the mothers are more competitive than the kids.

Aurelie just laughs. 'Yes, of course. You know what I mean, my poor two have everything against them: big bones, a clumsy mother, a father who can't tell a battement from a battlement... the list goes on. And then there's your little one, so tiny and she eats. How she eats! We've seen her eat.' She turns to Esme, her second in command, for confirmation, and she nods her assent, red curls bouncing.

'Well, you know they do have to keep their strength up, and if they turn professional they'll be dancing for ten hours a day, doing fifty performances a year. They can't risk damaging their bones by dieting too much. I know that Ria and I both ate plenty when we were their age.'

Aurelie looks taken aback by this sudden and surprising reference to my own experience. 'Well, you'd know best. Where was it you went again?'

'Walbrook Ballet School and then their company.' I offer the already well-known information, grudgingly.

'Yes, I remember now,' she says, bowing her crown of golden highlights over a pink plastic cooler emblazoned with the words, *Greedy Pig*, and alleviating it of its spoils: mini muffins, crudités, focaccia, a four pack of selected dips and packages of wafer thin meat. I'm surprised she's willing to tear herself away from watching her daughter's progress for long enough to talk to me, but then Lexie's status amongst the seniors largely depends on her mother's political manoeuvres behind the scenes.

'Can we entice you?' Esme calls out to a chorus of titters.

'Hmmm, yes, what about one of these spicy king prawns?' Aurelie extends the platter to me, her eyes flicking to the drumming of my restless fingers. 'Only thirty calories each,' she adds, as if that'll settle any possible argument I might counter.

'Thanks, but I'm allergic to shellfish.'

'Gosh, that must be a pain. However do you ever manage to dine out? Although, I know what you mean, I've got a terrible allergy to wheat.'

'But…' I trail off as we both look at the chunk of bread she is slathering with olive tapenade as we speak.

'But I usually just eat it anyway!' she says, with a bark of laughter as she bites into the crust. 'Yummy.'

With an effort I pull my attention back to the studio in front of me, *one detail at a time*, that's what I was taught to overcome the discomfort of pushing my body to incredible limits, *just concentrate on one detail at a time and before you know it the movement will be completed.*

Ria, my one-time competition and now my sister-in-law, perches on a stool in front of the mirrors at the far end of the studio, unable to do much more now her body is bent and twisted with arthritis. Yet her disability is of no matter here, because these girls know what she once was, the power that she once possessed to hold an audience in thrall. Every day when they enter the studio they witness the price Ria has paid for a few short years of transcending from normality to enchantment, her restless, ambitious spirit now trapped in a prematurely aged frame, but still it doesn't deter them. It is so very far off, there are years and years of schooling, of striving, or perhaps even adulation, before they retire in their late twenties or thirties and finally face the consequences of what this dream will do to them. Even Cass, who knows more of what Ria suffers than any of her friends, doesn't take it seriously, not as something that could happen to her.

Ria's expression is immutable, she has no sympathy for their little sufferings, their complaints about muscle spasms and bleeding toes, rather she is contemptuous of their weaknesses, because she knows only the strongest can escape the homogeneity of the corps de ballet and have the chance to stand alone. Her pupils respond to her words, to the critique in her gaze, moving as if they are one creature – all the disparate desires of the outside world wiped clean from their make-up free faces, thick curls and waves scraped back into identical buns, not a strand of hair permitted to fight loose from the pins and distract them from the pursuit of inhuman excellence.

But their clothing tells a different story. Leotards, tights, warm-up shorts, leggings and T-shirts are all fighting to show the originality of the wearer – the brighter, the tighter, the greater the urge to gain attention. *Look at me*, a shimmering pair of pink and orange leggings says, *look at what I can do.* Cass has genetics on her side and can afford to dress carelessly, pulling on whatever combination is clean five minutes before we leave the house, but there are others who aren't so fortunate. Strategically placed flowing cotton is used to disguise a barely perceptible swell of flesh, a softening around the waist, the betrayals of adolescence in the despised curves of breasts and thighs. This is only teamwork because it has to be that way. The real battles are fought between individuals. Each teen a gladiator, stretching her muscles and starving herself, to be at once weightless yet strong, delicate yet determined; each pair of pointe shoes supporting a violent nest of emotions contained in a cage of gently protruding bones.

I remove the lid from my take-away coffee. Aurelie and friends have been emailing everyone for weeks about going on a sponsored caffeine fast for July, *all money to go to our girls!* If I wasn't caffeinated most days I wouldn't be standing. My response? Colombian industrial strength ground. I liberate the aroma, blowing on it for good measure, and observe Aurelie's delicately snubbed nose wrinkling, identifying the contraband scent as she watches Cass's beautifully controlled développé through attitude into arabesque. If they told me they were making a stand against drugs I'd probably snort a line off one of their Tupperware boxes.

The girls are instructed to turn and repeat the exercise on the other side. Cass sees me and sticks her tongue out, before mouthing, 'go away', just as Lexie smiles at Aurelie and waves so enthusiastically that her breasts jiggle, testing the flimsy straps of her leotard in a very non-balletic way.

Aurelie pats me on the arm feigning reassurance, saying, 'Teenagers are a funny lot, aren't they? I expect she didn't mean it.' Knowing my daughter, she bloody did, and if I thought for a minute I'd get away with it I'd have probably mouthed some obscenity back, but that really would get me evicted.

Ria stands with difficulty as the girls form lines in the centre and she marks the enchaînement, her body unable to show them the full extent of what's required; but they've been doing this since they were three years old so they know the routine. Still, I recognise the regret in her face when they ask her questions and she has to call her assistant to join them from the children's class next door to demonstrate a perfect fouetté or tour jeté. I never wanted to be like Ria. I was always unsure about how much I was willing to give up, always wanting the best of everything, but Ria knew the sacrifices she needed to make and that for her at least, the dream was worth it. No, I could never have made the choices she did. And yet watching my daughter, her body gradually unfolding to the music like time-lapse footage of a familiar bloom rendered exotic under the scrutiny of the performance, I feel a twinge of envy. To be at the beginning of that journey again, for it all to be possible, yes, that I would seize with both hands.

Emma Victoria Miller writes contemporary and historical fiction. She has a PhD in literature from Durham University where she also teaches, and her work has been published in a numerous locations, including: NewWriting.Net, UEA140 Story, *Ariadne's Thread* and *The Feminist Wire*. She is a recipient of a Malcolm Bradbury Memorial Scholarship at UEA.

MATTHEW MOONEY

The Big Other

Extract from a novel.

MEN HATE CONDOMS BUT CAN'T ADMIT WHY. USUALLY OUR EXCUSE is the extra pressure they bring into the room, that half a minute interval to cordon everything off before the moment deflates. Although in this respect we don't help ourselves, the precursory 'just a sec' imposing the expectations, most of us have learnt to deal with it. Sometimes we'll say some crap about their sobering effect, that their creepy, synthetic feel is a timely reminder of why you should never think about what you're doing while you're having sex (it produces one of two outcomes, both an unsatisfactory and early finish). Justifications like these aren't right and I'm big enough to face the real reason: it's because they convert our efforts into something tangible, something comparable: data ready for analysis. It's because they renew the questions in the back of our minds: did we do enough? Did we win? Invariably the answer is no. But the truth is we could never drown out these phantom voices because all men fall short of what's asked of them, of the tasks we set ourselves. This is what the condom means to us.

Victoria reached into her bedside drawer and I knelt behind, desperate to annihilate the memory of her affair. They'd probably fucked loads and I hoped they had, 'just once' was always worse. 'Just once' played on the minds of all involved because a single, spectacular job left fantasies unharmed and desire unquenched. I needed to smooth out every wrinkle and obliterate her memory of the guy.

Folded over on her side with an unnaturally tanned leg jolted out, Victoria moaned as she strained her right hand and scratched through the drawer for a condom. The sounds jeered at me, stinging my groin.

She grimaced and kicked out at the duvet for balance. That generously freckled face had never shown me anything but mild satisfaction, so the more discomfort she displayed, the more I was sure the whole situation was my failing.

She was taking too long in her drawer. That fucking drawer. I hated that drawer. I'd never once seen inside it, and if I was honest I was thankful for this; her college pencil case of contraceptives, marked by Tipp-Ex of teenage fumbles, was enough additional anxiety on a normal evening. Whatever lurked beneath the rattling strips of pills and bottles of lotion would only demonstrate new inadequacies – ignorance I was in no shape to explore.

A droop-on isn't normally a big deal as long as it is approached with confidence, dealt with up front. But as I felt weakness creep up my thighs, I tried to counteract gravity by tensing my arse cheeks.

'No,' I said.

'What?'

'Take your time won't you?' I tried to joke but it came out sharper than I'd intended.

She turned round, and without looking directly at me, tossed the pen-purse between my cold thighs. 'What's wrong?'

Well the answer was obvious: some guy had wedged his way into my love life, attaining that sought after accolade of balls deep. Congratulations pal, you've fucked me too.

I swallowed at the air. 'Nothing. Just tired.'

In business-like silence she lurched over, laid me back (which only added to my frustration) and went to work. I tried to stop Victoria by gently pulling her up but this movement was counterintuitive – men are brought up with the image of fellatio basically being a push south against a certain amount of resistance, so my effort was rather half-arsed. Like most being fucked over, to protect the ego, I presumed I was up against some Greek god, a ripped and bronzed Adonis tearing his way through my girlfriend behind my back. Now this was quite natural. I told myself there was nothing I could have done to prevent it and I calmed down. This was until I realised that such a guy wouldn't be getting sucked off so passively.

Even if Victoria resuscitated me, in my eyes I'd already failed – I wasn't supposed to need her help. Quite the opposite. It was clear from the way she went on wincing in disgust that she very much agreed with me: our relationship was dead. Ejaculation educates the mind to fear death, each *petite mort* teaches us in real life to hold off just a little longer. With my own expiration (in both senses) anywhere but near, what seemed worse to me was being forgotten. You can have a relationship go to shit as long as you're the one they think of each night some paunchy estate agent red-faces from behind. You've got to admire those old men whose wives hold out for years long after they've croaked it. Maybe that's the ultimate goal, fuck off early but leave a hole so gaping it can't be fixed by anyone else. But this would never happen with Victoria and this realisation cut like hell. When I died I wanted Victoria at my funeral reading my eulogy to a hall of friends and family, to a full room of faceless grey blurs, because that's how you measure someone's worth: by how crowded and sad it is at the end, by how long after you've gone people speak your name. Victoria gagged and swept hair from her mouth, and I figured my buffet had better be a good one.

'Listen, I can't do this,' she said.

'Well, look, you don't have to, we'll just put on a film or something.'

'No, Edward. This.' She stuck out her neck, and with her hand gestured back and forth at the space between us. 'Me and you.'

I couldn't believe it; she'd got in there before me. Fucking somebody else I could have dealt with (albeit eventually); be the bigger man, open my arms and say, 'come home, get back to me, I'll make you forget him,' but for stripping me of all ammunition I'd never forgive her. To add to the insult I felt my dick getting predictably hard.

'What? Why?' These questions were as stupid as her one earlier.

Victoria leaned over to switch on the bedside lamp and I smelt her warm hair as the curls shook against her right cheek, sparking a memory I couldn't place.

'Look, Edward—'

'Is there someone else?'

'Jesus. I think you should go.'

I wanted to grab the face of the Adonis and push my thumbs into his sockets until he cried for me to stop. I wanted to smash it. To shatter it and roll Victoria's arching back across the shards. I wanted to cause her some damage if I had to leave.

'There's someone else, isn't there?' I knew this insecurity was unattractive but I couldn't help myself.

'Look, just go will you?'

'It's someone else.'

'There's no one else.'

'Can't I stay, it's nearly one?' I figured if I could hang around, I'd be able to change her mind.

She pulled on a T-shirt I didn't recognise. 'You're on the couch out there if you stay.'

Kingsland High Street was pissed-up and I hailed a black cab; I was still partially asleep or maybe half-cut from the wine at dinner, either way too tired and ashamed for public transport. The cab winked orange to pull in while fag ash from the dank pavement burnt my nose.

'Crouch End, mate.'

Thankfully the cabbie started talking on his phone so I dozed in the back. Victoria had eventually kicked me out because I'd tried to sneak back into her room after a strategic (and agonising) half an hour wait. I'd tried playing the sympathy card – crying as I walked in. Shit, what had led me to think this was the quality play I'll never know. But I shuffled in saying her name as meekly as I could. In fact that wasn't the hard part, the whole act came surprisingly easy to me, to the point I began to doubt whether it was an act at all. Was I actually this upset about the whole thing? I'd decided that this couldn't be confirmed either way, and that it was probably best for me just to nip the whole thing in the bud there and then by any means possible. Obviously it hadn't worked, it had just pissed her off, and this was why I was in a cab on my own.

The Adonis was probably round there, fucking her awake right this second. It amazed me just how quickly you could be forgotten when you were alive. I smeared the condensation on the window to look at the metronomic passing of the streetlights thrusting by. I'd done really well tonight; I'd failed tremendously. Undoubtedly my behaviour would get around. Victoria would be vlogging tomorrow and it was a matter of time until her friends (my friends) knew all about my behaviour. It would spread through work. Any chance of rebound poon was simply off the cards. My only hope would be that the Adonis would fix her so well that she'd forget the whole evening. I swallowed the taste of salt. Go on son.

Matthew Mooney was born in Huddersfield in 1985. Before embarking on postgraduate studies, he toured in a punk band for six years. In 2010 he studied an MA in Critical and Cultural Theory. Now studying at UEA, he is currently working on his first novel, *The Big Other*. He is also a support worker for a man with a brain injury.

SARAH MOORE

London Traffic

Chapter 1

'I SUPPOSE IT'S SAFE TO LET YOU COME IN?'

These are his first ever words to me. Sardonic, of course; spoken with humour, but flecked, I come to realise later, with vigilance.

I am standing on his doorstep; the shoes I bought on Oxford Street at the weekend have rubbed a blister into my left heel, while a red leather satchel containing the papers for Friday's team meeting is slung across my chest. My face must register shock or anxiety, or possibly both, because his shoulders immediately drop, he laughs and pushes the door further open so that a mechanical drone from a radio or television spills onto the pavement.

'I'm sorry. A joke; a bad one. Come in.'

Although it is summer, the tenth of June to be precise (you see how the date will stick with me) an abstract, city dusk has fallen. An invisible sun is slipping beneath the earth, the air turning mauve as cars and buildings light up like fairground rides. A few doors further up the street a couple is leaving one of those ubiquitous pasta places. An argument drifts over their retreating footsteps.

'I didn't,' the man protests, 'I was only checking the train times to Manchester.'

I am tired. I was caught by Maggie as I headed for the lifts, fell asleep on the tube, got off at Acton Town instead of East Acton, and then spent a fruitless twenty minutes trying to follow the directions I had scribbled on a yellow Post-it note before I noticed my mistake.

'I'm Bruce,' he says, because I haven't moved. 'Bruce Tyler.' And he holds out his hand.

I can't help but stare at him. He is quite old, mid-forties, I guess; dark hair with threads of grey that flatter rather than age, brown eyes and a strong, tanned face suggestive of travel and money and instantly more compelling than the milky complexions of my civil service colleagues. He is mid-height and wearing jeans with a white, immaculately laundered shirt that looks like it belongs behind a suit but is unbuttoned at the neck, and he is cradling a large glass of red wine.

'Really,' he adds, 'I don't bite.' He gestures at the wine. 'I opened this a while ago. I got a little bored waiting for you.' He smiles again, but when another moment passes a frown begins to crease the space above his nose. Actually, I'm not reacting to what he's said. At the time, I barely register the oddity of his opening remark. The reason I am paralysed, rooted to a spot between the bins and a tub of shabby geraniums, is because he looks exactly like an older, more sophisticated, version of Daniel. Finally, I shake myself, mutter an apology – something about work and getting lost – and then I step over the threshold.

Inside the place is striking, just as I was promised on the telephone. He's gutted the entire ground floor to make it one big space, the kitchen at the far end with white cupboards and grey tiles, the front all taupe carpet and magnolia woodwork. Bookshelves have been fitted either side of the fireplace. One has been modified to accommodate a flat-screen television and somewhere on the far side of the world racing cars are screaming around in tarmac circles. He walks over to the television, switches it off, and we are stranded suddenly in the middle of an awkward silence.

'A glass of wine?' He angles the bottle over an empty glass, pauses and cocks his head to one side. 'Or perhaps you're the type who doesn't drink during the week?' He is teasing me already, his voice a singer's baritone with an accent that slices square the end of his words. I should feel uncomfortable or patronised, instead, absurdly, I am flattered at his familiarity. I take the glass and let him lead me towards the back of the house.

He maintains a steady chatter; where he has sourced this fabric, why he used Romo rather than Sanderson, or Ross rather than Conran. The names trip from his tongue like family members. I open cupboard doors, run my hand along the breakfast bar, and ask the usual questions about how long he's lived here and whether the roof is OK and are there any damp problems, but by the time I follow him upstairs I already want to buy the house so badly I am formulating phrases I can use with Edward, stamping down the knot of guilt that has settled in my stomach.

Four doors lead from the landing. First, at the front, he shows me the main bedroom, awash with creams and pale yellow. Next a room that is perfect for a cot – though instinctively I choose not to draw attention to the ring on my finger, my soon-to-be wedding. The third door he opens with a flourish. Inside is a bathroom. The bath, the size of a bed, is sunk into black marble, the shower has a vertical line of body-jets and a floor-length mirror along the inside wall. Standing in the doorway I find I am blushing and whether it is association, premonition, or simply the effects of alcohol on an empty stomach, is impossible to tell. In any case, Bruce has already moved towards the other, fourth, room. Here the door is slightly ajar, the darkness inside diluted by the soft gleam of a nightlight. He holds it a little further open to reveal twin beds and two child-size forms nestled under duvets. Without him doing anything, I understand that I am not to go in.

'Normally my ex-wife has custody of them,' he says. And shuts the door.

Back downstairs, he tops up our glasses and sits on a beige leather sofa. He gestures at the facing one.

'So Claire, what do you think?'

I take another mouthful of wine, buying time, but I cannot see a reason not to tell him. I explain that Edward and I have agreed to buy a house already, from an elderly couple who are moving in with their son; that the price has been agreed and solicitors instructed; that I only came to view the house because his agent was so insistent. I hear my words, earnest and concerned – and empty. I stop and he smiles, clearly amused.

'But you did come didn't you, Claire?' When I say nothing, he raises his eyebrows encouragingly, as if he is prompting a child in a nativity play. I nod slowly, caught moth-like by his gaze. I think, this is how Daniel will look in twenty years' time, but I won't be the one to see it. 'And you have no legal obligation to buy the other property?' Bruce continues. I shake my head obediently. 'Well then…' He shrugs dismissively, reaches for the bottle, and begins to ask me questions about my work.

An hour later, I am still talking. We have covered the Department – its external and internal politics – my home, even Edward. It will turn out, of course, that he was sizing me up – assessing my potential – but at the time it really seemed as if he found me entertaining, even charming, possibly attractive. Curled within a golden pool of meticulous lighting,

SARAH MOORE

the hideous shoes kicked beneath the sofa, I am feeling quite loquacious. There is no stopping me, although my enunciation, thickened by wine, requires increasing attention. I am still in full flow when he glances, rather obviously, at his watch.

'Goodness,' he says.

I look at my watch too. 'Goodness,' I repeat. I gather my things in a clumsy rush. At the door, there is a large rectangular mirror set within an ornately carved frame. I see my face, flushed along the cheekbones, my dark-blonde hair, flat like feathered wings against the sides of my too-thin face, my eyes which are green, and the rather rumpled cloth of my brown jacket. Bruce assumes I am staring at the mirror.

'It's beautiful, isn't it?' he says. 'Spanish. From before the civil war.' He runs a proprietary finger around the edge of a pale walnut rose petal.

'Yes,' I say, and touch the mirror too. And then, because he seems to expect more, I add, rather blandly, 'How lovely to own something so special.'

Back in our rented flat, Edward is reluctant but ultimately persuadable. Within a week we withdraw our other offer. I send the elderly couple a bunch of flowers and a careful, handwritten note expressing the hope that they soon find new buyers.

Three weeks later I come back from lunch to find Agatha bent over my desk, peering at something through blacked-rimmed glasses. She steps smartly to one side as I approach.

'Your phone has been bleeping, Claire.'

It's lying on top of a document entitled *Waste Recycling, Treatment and Disposal Sites* only I know it was left underneath the file, which is why I didn't see it when I gathered my things. Now, miraculously freed from its papery covers, a text message is pasted in the middle of the screen.

Claire – call me. Bruce

I wonder, momentarily, how he got my number, but assume the solicitors must have given it to him. Agatha watches as I zip the phone into the side-pocket of my bag. She has the desk opposite mine, they butt onto each other divided only by a low Perspex screen. If my gaze strays from my computer I sometimes find myself looking straight into Agatha's round, pale-blue eyes, and when my telephone rings I become aware of the sudden hush, the fixed set of Agatha's shoulders, and the gentle fingering of her papers so that not a word is missed. Recently I have taken to conducting my personal telephone conversations in the toilets.

'Go on,' I dare her silently, 'ask me who Bruce is.' But she won't have the nerve. Agatha is in her thirties, single, and wears A-line skirts from Marks and Spencer that fall a good inch below her knees. I suspect that we are not so far apart, she and I; the difference is mainly Edward, and a finger's width of fine wool cloth.

After about forty-five minutes, I pick up my bag and head for the ladies'. The building where I work is in the heart of London. It boasts an elegant stone façade and overlooks a back street near Tottenham Court Road. But it, too, has been gutted. The work areas surround the central lift shaft and are arranged into a series of open-plan stations separated by full-height partitions. When I first arrived I would often circumnavigate the entire floor without managing to identify my desk amongst the maze of wood veneer. This time I find my way without incident, passing en route a meeting room, though possibly 'room' is inapt to describe the transparent, box-like structure in question. Inside, I can see my colleagues; one is jabbing his pen at the points of a graph. The others have the glazed expression of passengers on a long-haul flight. One of them, Lucy, catches my eye and briefly taps three fingers to her lips. I pull a sympathetic face.

I tell myself the call is about something tedious, possibly the Land Registry or the seller's questionnaire. Nevertheless, I can feel my heart quickening in anticipation of the conversation. The ladies' is empty. Absurdly, I check my hair in the mirror before I stand at the window and locate his number, the traffic a silent, metallic, river below. He answers just as I am steeling myself for the disappointment of voicemail.

There is a fraction of a second where he is still speaking with someone else, and then, 'Claire!'

I get a warm feeling in my stomach, as if I have swallowed a mouthful of brandy.

'Can you come round to the house tonight? After work?' His voice is light but has surprising urgency.

Sarah Moore lives in Norfolk with her husband and teenage children. After graduating from Cambridge she spent many years at the London Bar, but now combines writing with judicial work. *London Traffic* is a crime novel. Her other project, *The Switch*, is a novel set in wartime and present-day Norfolk.

MOLLY MORRIS

Charades

The following is an excerpt from a novel, in which Phoebe Elm must return home after learning her family is one of their town's lottery winners. The big prize? For one weekend only, they can bring someone back from the dead. They choose her father.

W E DRIVE TO THE LAKE IN SILENCE, LOUISE AT THE WHEEL, OUR mother in the front seat, me wedged in the back; the tension swells within the tiny four-door like a broken leg, as Hatchett County whisks by, cornfields thick as clouds of bees. The letter the City sent Louise said the boat would arrive around ten, bringing with it the hundred chosen 'formerly-deceased,' including our father. On the dash in fat, blue lines, the clock reads that we've only got nine minutes.

Louise pulls into the Canorak Country Club parking lot, an expanse of forty or so camper-sized spaces in front of a creamy yellow mansion we could never afford a membership to. The front-facing window reveals a glass chandelier the size of the car; on the other side is the lake, bulging along the horizon.

'Do you need to be a member to park here?' I ask, as I slam my car door shut and hike my purse up my shoulder. A button on the strap nestles into my collarbone.

Mom adjusts the straw hat teetering on her head. 'Who cares?' she says.

We cut along the path stretching from the club to the docks, pussy willows sprouting up in a swarm that almost reaches my waist. Lake Canorak is blurred with an ominous mist that stretches skyward, shielding any boats or sea monsters lurking more than twenty feet from shore. The landscape is like two bickering panels: a grey fog on the bottom, trickling up to a serene blue sky that leaves the remainder of Hatchett County sparkling. Lake Canorak is never this murky in the summertime and I can't help but think Dad will be especially unimpressed. He'll roll his eyes and mutter, 'Couldn't they have gotten a fan? Fireworks?' He and his fellow undead passengers could only come back once every ten years, and goddamn it, he'd say, the lake was more depressing than their funerals.

I squint my eyes at the muddled water. Anything could be hiding behind the mist: a wooden corner, the rounded sheen of a bubble, a scaly tail. But I'm really looking for him, for anything suggesting he's just behind the fog, watching. Waiting. In minutes, he'll be here again, feet planted into the wood of the dock, hands resting on his belt loops. Will his heart beat? Will his flesh dangle from his limbs, torso covered in dirt, eyes a milky white? The last time I'd spoken to him was the last time I'd looked him in the eyes, over four years ago, when he'd picked me up from the police station as I roiled in a plastic chair, the taste of seven mai tais still coating my tongue like a wool blanket. It was everything he could ever want: further proof I was his lowlife kid, and not just some idiot with an equally idiotic boyfriend, 'having a good time,' like I insisted. Like I was. His jaw had shuddered with rage and his irises were red-rimmed, as if the blood vessels splattered like spoiled tomatoes. He hadn't left the house in weeks, his hair all but completely gone, the skin under his eyes twin empty parachutes, but he was irate enough to peel into the station at four in the morning. If he didn't, someone might see me. What would he do then?

I was so shocked to find him swaying in the police station doorway I thought the neon-colored drinks I'd glugged were spurring hallucinations. He was so sick. The doctors at St Gerard's only found the tumor nestled above his brain stem a few months before because he'd fallen in the street outside his shop and someone called an ambulance, which was bad enough. Did they have any idea how much ambulances cost? Moron do-gooders. And did the paramedics really have to turn the sirens on? It was all he could talk about as he lay in the hospital, body woven with translucent tubes so he looked like a twenty-tentacled octopus.

The lump was the size of a golf ball, growing rapidly – an invasion of cells doctors couldn't keep at bay, as if it were thousands of rebel soldiers charging across crab grass at Gettysburg. They would attempt surgery, but it probably wouldn't help. Too progressed, as it was. C'est la vie. He was given the one-year-to-live stamp, maybe less. And they were right: one year, almost to the day, and he was gone. It would only take him nine months to slip into an irreversible coma. Only Mom had the courage to feel shocked when he died.

The path finally reaches the dock, which is so cluttered with people I can barely pick apart each head. A group by the water dons matching 'Welcome Home Mom!' T-shirts while another holds tightly to clusters of balloons. One family has brought a series of square posters, each with a different red and orange striped letter that spells out: 'WE MISSED U.' Just where the boat will dock, there's a brass band bumping and burping a sped-up rendition of *Yankee Doodle Dandy*.

We didn't even bring flowers. I spent the morning standing in front of Louise's floor-length mirror, tugging at the hem of the only dress I brought, willing it to reach my knees. Dad's voice and what he might say upon seeing me echoed in my head: 'Is that really what you're wearing?' When I mentioned it to Louise she said I ought to have a little more faith. Four years of death could do wonders to a person.

But why change now? He'd kept the shtick up for fifty-eight years.

'Do you think he'll look dead?' I ask. 'Like, right out of the grave?' Is it his body or his soul that comes back? Both?

Louise shrugs. 'He's supposed to come back like he left.'

'A vegetable?'

My mother's head snaps up so fast, her hat slips off her head, revealing a tuft of white-blonde hair held back in a butterfly clip. 'You watch your mouth,' she says as her fingers flutter upwards to catch the straw brim.

'I'm just saying,' I say as I raise my hands. 'Has anyone really thought this out? What if his skin is green, or his fingers are falling off?' Memories of the two Welcome Back Weekends I've been alive for are clean white gaps in the folds of my brain. We didn't go to the parade or family picnics on Lake Canorak, because why would we? We didn't win. The dead blended in; but then, it's hard to tell the dead from the living in Hatchett County on a good day.

'Then I'll collect them in the bathtub,' Mom says. 'We'll figure it out.'

I bite the corner of my lip, Dad's big return playing out like a scene we've rehearsed for weeks: he'll saunter down the docks, hands in his pockets with his thumbs plucked forward. He'll look to Mom, to me, to Louise. He'll lean in and give us each a shoulder-heavy hug, scanning Mom for new jewelry, Louise for a hickey, my breath for something cheap. Same old, same old. When I'll say I moved to Los Angeles after he died – *the land of dreams, Dad!* – that I've stumbled into acting and landed a reasonable part or two – *I've even got an understudy, Dad!* – and that I'm so clean my ears squeak – *Percocet? That's for back pain, not excessive recreational use!* – he'll peel down my ears to look for dirt.

As if on cue, the crowd breaks into cheering, elbows jutting into sides as people clamor for a closer look at the lake. The mist has parted in half. Only a hundred or so feet from shore, a boat with the words *Heaven Sent* scrawled on the side has appeared. It's as if it's fallen from the sky without so much as a ripple. The boat cuts through the water with ease, hovering almost, moving faster than birds slicing the sky. I don't have time to swallow before it reaches the dock, ropes lassoing out to the posts as the band shuffles into the crowd, a tuba croaking out one last welcoming burp. Someone has only just thrust a plank outward, connecting the boat to the dock, when the boat's side door swings open and a woman emerges. A high voice from somewhere in the crowd lets out an exasperated whoop.

'They're coming out,' I say, no louder than a whisper. My heart chugs with thick beats as if someone's pounding my ribcage with a steel hammer.

Men and women file out in a thin trail from the door, slinking onto the dock and fanning out in search of their families. They don't look dead, not really, but each one dons a get-up fit for senior prom or an especially flashy church lunch. Most have on white gloves or slick suits, pearls and cravats, except for one man, who's wearing overalls.

'Do you see him?' Mom asks. 'Is he there?'

We each crane our necks, bodies balancing on tiptoes. 'There!' Louise shouts as she pats my shoulder with frantic taps. 'He's there, at the bottom.'

I narrow my eyes to where the tip of her finger leads, gaze flicking from face to face until I pause on the balding head I somehow convinced myself I'd just about forgotten. 'Is he wearing a tuxedo?' I ask.

He bobs through the crowd, in search of whoever's brought him here. Does he know it's us? What if he's looking for that woman? Louise has begun waving with both hands, flapping her arms like a rabid crow.

'Here he comes, here he comes,' she says as she pets the waist of her dress.

It's him, ambling up the docks, it's him nudging through a tearful family who has, for whatever reason, broken into applause. And then he's here, standing in the blank space where the crowd has split. He shrugs his shoulders to peel off the black suit hugging his frame and lifts a hand to finger the bowtie settled at the center of his neck. His skin is a healthy peach, etched with fewer worried wrinkles than I remember, his gaze darting between us with wide, bright blinks.

Only when I tilt my face to my mother, to my sister, do I realize my jaw is hanging open. Are we waiting for him to speak? Mom and Louise stay silent, eyes wild as if they're staring into headlights. Dad's eyes don't dip below our faces, leaving my dress, Louise's neck, my mother's wrists, unexamined. I knee out the dress, fluttering the hem. Doesn't he want to see?

A beat passes before I clear my throat and say, 'Is that the tux we buried you in?'

'For Christ's sake Phoebe,' Mom hisses. 'Not now.'

'Must be,' Louise whispers. It's still as crisp as it was for his funeral.

Nobody stretches out so much as a fingertip. Dad pulls at his starched shirtsleeves before sweeping out his hands and raising his eyebrows into expectant arches. 'Hi dolls,' he practically shouts as he waggles his fingers, beckoning us into his embrace. His voice, high and wiry, practically cuts the clouds. He's actually smiling, his teeth wide as gum and pricked with sunlight. 'Anyone know where I can get a steak?'

Molly Morris is a California native with a penchant for the bizarre. She is currently in the throes of her first novel, plus a short story collection, whose settings range from snow globes to a Superstition Crisis Centre, from a cannibalism-themed theme park to a bayou town overridden with mummies.

KATHLEEN MOURA

São Paulo Riviera

Prologue

EDUARDO IS TIRED. HE'S BEEN MAKING DOGS FOR TEN HOURS. HE LEANS out of the van, elbows on his serving hatch. The river is pink, rippling grey – the sun a red-rimmed shimmer beyond. The club behind is buzzing thickly. Everyone who was going home has gone home. The kids in there now won't be out for hours and they won't want a dog. They'll just be gazing and chewing, clutching round for a fag or a zoot or gum.

Chico turns off the funk that has been pumping through the van's sound system. Eduardo rolls his eyes in thanks.

'Elis?' Chico says, flicking through his phone.

'I won't tell anyone,' Eduardo says. 'It's our secret.'

Chico puts on his old, camp bossa nova. He takes a plastic stool, moves it into the orange light of the serving hatch, the dawn around still soupy. He lights up a zoot, leans back and closes his eyes. His face drops and his youth shows. Eduardo likes his boss, in moments like this, when he isn't pretending to be a gangster, dressed up in gold, surrounded by his girls and his mates and his uncles. When he is just a kid that likes Elis and smoking, smoking to Elis.

Eduardo turns back to the van, to the frying pan on the hob, ignoring the mess; the debris of rolls, the trodden-down sausages, the dark dried streaks of ketchup. He stirs his sauce with a wooden spoon. His special Japanese sauce. The one Chico has ordered him to make, to impress his new girlfriend. It's thick and it glistens, Eduardo tries to take a sniff, tries to find the smell amongst the rotting stink of the river.

'What the fuck do they put in that river? It smells like shit, or something,' he calls out.

'Dunno man,' said Chico. 'Looks nicer than the traffic though, right?'

The cars are there all around them; Eduardo can hear their roar. He can hear the city waking, feel the flickering of a new day. Babies wailing, dogs barking, concrete groaning against the heat. Not even daybreak and everything already crying, roaring, screaming to be heard. Everything but the river, which makes no sound.

'It's dead man, that's why it stinks, it's dead,' says Eduardo.

He goes back to his pan. It looks about ready. Tomato ketchup, lemon, soy sauce. Eduardo doesn't know much about Japan, he doesn't think Chico does either, but he knows they use soy sauce. He licks some off a spoon.

'It's good, Chico. You want to taste it?' he calls out.

'Yeah, go on,' Chico says.

'On a dog?' Eduardo asks.

'Yeah, why not?'

Eduardo prepares a dog for his boss, taking more care then he has done all night. He feels sorry for Chico, sometimes. He's a good guy, but it's so hard to be good in São Paulo. The guns, the cars. The money – the absence of money. Eduardo hands the dog to Chico who is stoned now, beatific looking, baseball cap off to the side. He smells, from the club, from the dancing he does but doesn't like.

'You got to change that shirt before Melissa comes back,' says Eduardo.

'It's the river man, it's not me.'

'You can't blame everything on the river. Eat the dog.'

Chico closes his little pebble eyes, stretches out his chubby cheeks and takes a dreamy bite. He chews. He opens his eyes.

'Fuck man. Fuck it's good. You got it. You got it. It tastes like the sauces they have there. In Japan,' Chico says.

'Chico, you never been to Japan,' says Eduardo.

'Whatever. She's gonna fucking love it man.'

Eduardo smiles. The sun is turning yellow and his shirt is already damp with the heat. Soon the whole city will be sweating, the concrete baking, the blue sky unremitting and vast. Another hot day. But a good dawn, a good end to a night's work. He stretches and yawns. He can hear the wheezy roar of a bus, louder, heavier than the cars. He should get going, before they get packed out and he has to stand all the way home.

Chico jumps up. He's excited. He's stoned and excited and his gold chains jangle.

'Eddie, this is it. This is what we're gonna have when we're in the Riviera. You're gonna come with me. You'll come to the Riviera too,' he says.

Sofia's eyes are gritty. Her body feels sticky, unnerved. She woke up at two and now it's five-thirty. She sits on the balcony in her nightdress, looking down at the twinkling sprawl, going on and on and on. She fingers her phone. Her daughter is not back yet and didn't pick up when she called. She's dancing somewhere, Sofia tells herself, scanning the city stretched out before her, wondering under which twinkling globe her daughter has been flicking her hair and biting her lip and rolling her eyes. A night bus, stopping and starting, comes down from the North and she hopes Melissa is on board.

It's a relentless city, beautiful at dawn, when the seething hot mess of it is still disguised, when the lights still glitter, red and white, and the sky is dark and tacky, lilac and blue. Soon it will be all grey, grey, yellow – smog and concrete and a piercing tormenting sun. The streetlights will blink off and a stream of gleaming cars will appear. The air will hang heavy with horns and there will be an underlying grumbling roar that reminds Sofia of the sound of the sea.

The night bus has reached the river. Sofia has watched it, waiting like this, many times. She is lucky, in some ways, to be able to do so. Her apartment is on the nineteenth floor. Nothing hides the city, stretched out in front of her. The newer apartment buildings are enormous and would eclipse her own, but they are being built behind, near the avenue, not on her strip of road. Sometimes, though, Sofia wished she didn't know how far the city went on, wished her fears had less ground on which to roam.

A ringing thump echoes through the air. It drives itself through Sofia's tired skull. She winces. The foundations for the new tower block are already being pounded down. The construction company has moved fast; there's a 'sold out' banner across their poster of a happy family, eating dinner. But they shouldn't be working now; there is a law against building this early, before seven. Sofia hears a baby crying from some apartment in the next door block, then the chuk chuk chuk of a helicopter, a black wasp on the orange sky.

So many people in so little space. How can they squeeze in anyone else? She's watched São Paulo grow and grow, on and on and now up and up and up. It scares her, sometimes, how mammoth it has become, and her right at the centre of it. Sofia stands up and stretches. At least she has the sky and its colours, the pink and the black, the bleached white and the blue, the exhausted, pretty gold at the end of the day.

She leans out of the balcony to see if the bakery is open yet. It is; there's Fabio, setting out the red plastic tables in the soot-grey street, the glow of the bar behind him. And there is the night bus pulling up, stopping. When it moves on Sofia sees Melissa, standing on the pavement, her tight white dress riding up her leg. Sofia closes her eyes, breathes out, waves to her daughter. Melissa doesn't see her, doesn't glance up at her home, she's hugging Fabio in her over-friendly way.

Sofia makes a small plan: to wash and change, go down for sweet coffee and fried bread. She'll tell Melissa off for staying out so late. Fabio will make clucking, calming noises. He'll pour refills into their tiny glasses and Melissa will eat two or three slices of his breakfast cake. Then Sofia will get on the road to work, before the heaving morning rush, jittery and scratchy from the coffee and the night hours, but having at least breakfasted with her sweaty, smelly, beautiful daughter. She knows she will laugh a few times before seven am. That must be something, she thinks.

Hector is on the morning shift at Tiete transport hub, cleaning the night buses. They always need more work than the day shift. They arrive at Tiete scrawled with graffiti; black tags, fluorescent shapes, messages from the night kids. He fills a bucket full of soapy water and starts with the green 478-10. He knows this bus route well. It starts on Avenida Paulista, and travels, stopping and starting, down through Rua da Consalação and out across Perdizes, on under the mean, dripping, fly-over Minhacão, stopping at Barra Funda metro. It goes up behind Arcade Park before heading through the North zone, to the favela Brasilandia. He can see it all now, in his mind's eye, the shopping crowds on Paulista, the suited men, the cheap drugstores. The graffiti over Consalação cemetery, angels peering out at the road; the flower sellers opposite, by the hospital. The crackheads and homeless, partying, dying, by fires under the flyover. The quiet middle class streets with trees and tiles and security guards. The concrete sprawl of the favela, the danger, the guns, the hissing teeth.

Hector travelled that bus route for years and others too. Hector knows the veins of the city, the textures of its streets. He knows the dusty palms and the bright green shoots which creep, despite themselves, into the cracks in the concrete and blossom there. He knows the tarry hot smells of particular drains and where to suck in the scent of night jasmine. He knows the stink of the river, the sad decaying river, which cuts through the city.

East zone, West zone, North zone, South zone. He knows it all, he feels it all, even now: the stop and breath of the bus, the wheeze of the road, the currents of cars, the tidal traffic, the lapping pavements. Most of all he knows the people: the sallow faces, the smiles, the jokes, the dark eyes, the murmuring gossip. He sees the drip, drip, drip of the city making its mark on his passengers. They are weary in the morning sun but wired and alive when journeying out into the garish neon lights.

'This one, it's bad inside,' says the driver, rubbing his eyes, loping down off the bus.

'What happened?' Hector asks.

'We had a hold-up, near Brasilandia.'

Hector closes his eyes. His son works in Brasilandia; it could have been his son's bus. He figures out the timings in his head. João would be fine, if he went training after work, as he often does.

'Blood?' he asks.

'No. They were cool. Just the phones and the money. One girl had a laptop.'

'Piss?'

The driver nods.

'Stinks in there.'

Hector groans. He turns back to the shed. He'll need bleach.

São Paulo Riviera is a novel that traverses the urban sprawl of Brazil, trying to discover what is required to live and survive there. **Kathleen Moura** is about to begin a Chase-funded creative critical PhD at UEA on megacity fiction – how infrastructure and architecture affect the art produced in the world's biggest cities.

RADHIKA OBEROI

The Taxonomy of Soy Sauce

Pig kidneys in a cider and mustard sauce

XIUYING ZOU RIPPED OPEN THE CELLOPHANE COVER ON A PACK OF British Pig Kidneys with her meat-and-poultry knife and transferred its contents onto a chopping board. Her knife sliced the kidneys into halves and diced the meat, gleaming with lard and droplets of moisture, into pieces that measured three centimetres each. With the precision of a surgeon, she guided her knife through the tender flesh, trimming each portion of excess fat until the pieces lay in neat rows on the chopping board, awaiting the inevitability of being sautéed in a frying pan over a gentle heat.

'Testicles,' she announced suddenly, addressing herself to Marina Martinez, her Brazilian flatmate, who was stirring a saucepan full of fusilli spirals. 'If these were British pig testicles, I would chop-chop-chop and eat raw,' she continued, cutting the last piece of meat with the vehemence of a butcher pulverising a tough and unyielding animal.

Xiuying's irrelevant reference to a pig's privates while cooking kidneys in a mustard and cider sauce confirmed what Marina suspected – the affair had ended and it had ended badly. She chose not to say anything for the moment, and fixed her eyes on the fusilli, bloating up to acquire the wholesome features of a quick-and-tasty lunch, as promised on the cardboard box that contained the pasta. She stirred the saucepan on the hob with a steadfast devotion to the food boiling inside it, as Xiuying raved on, flailing her arms through a cloud of wholegrain mustard, crushed garlic and black pepper that thickened around her as she spoke.

'My ma warned me – "Stay away from foreigners," she said to me on Skype. She knew Kevin was a porky; she knew he would break my heart.' Xiuying snapped a stalk of celery to demonstrate – a small incision of casual flirting had cut the chambers of her cardiac muscle into perfect, irredeemable halves.

'I knew something was wrong when he wouldn't make eye contact with me,' said Xiuying, pouring two tablespoons of sunflower oil into a frying pan.

Kevin's eyes were like century eggs, she had once said to her flatmates as they sat and ate around a dining table that resembled a food atlas, with roasts, gravies, bakes and stir-fried flora and fauna that mocked geographical boundaries and cultural authenticity. His eyes were the colour of duck egg yolks that had been preserved in a muddy mixture of clay, ash and quicklime for several months. A mossy green, flecked with grey – liquid irises like fermented yolks. Those irises had silently lied to her, stealthily cheated on her, and permanently shifted their unreliable gaze upon other romantic attractions.

Xiuying emptied a bowl of chopped onions into the pan that was sizzling with oil. The onions crackled and spat some oil on her face. She moved a few inches away from the hob but continued to fry the foul-smelling, temperamental mix, till the circular pieces were scorched a warm caramel. She added the meat to the onions and dropped a swirl of butter into the pan, muttering as she sautéed.

'He dumps me – the suckling pig – and I stand here cooking his favourite dish,' she said to Marina, whose pasta was ready, and who was planning a furtive exit from the flat's common kitchen. 'He dumps me, and I make his food; I will eat these British Pig Kidneys all alone, but with him in my head, talking, always talking about his football, his new jersey, the cheerleaders… oh that wild boar!'

The meat cooked while she ranted and was nearly burnt before she salvaged it with her cider and mustard sauce. She allowed it to simmer for a few minutes before taking it off the hob and banging the frying pan onto the dining table.

'It is ready Marina,' she said, pointing at the frying pan with theatrical flair. 'Now tell, how can I eat it alone? How can I eat it without thinking of *him*?'

'Riu-yiing,' said Marina, mangling her flatmate's name with her Hispanic accent. 'Just splash soy sauce on the kidneys. Then it becomes a new dish – *your dish* – that won't remind you of him,' she advised before leaving the kitchen with her pasta.

'Soy sauce,' mumbled Xiuying, staring at the space in the kitchen that Marina had filled, with newfound reverence. 'It will ruin the dish but cure the pain *here*.' She put her right hand across her chest and stared at the food.

Fusilli with Basil, Tomatoes and Avocado Sauce

Marina Martinez was unusually reticent while Xiuying raged about her failed affair with Kevin. She was fretting over her avocado sauce. Ever since she had arrived in England from Bahia, and had moved into a student residence on the vast, emerald campus of her university, she had been distressed by her own inability to replicate the taste and texture of Brazilian food. She had laboured over a vatapá, but the thick paste of bread, shrimp and coconut milk she had cooked lacked the velvety smoothness or the cheeky pungency that she was accustomed to. Even a simple beans-and-rice had caused tears of shame and homesickness to fall into the saucepan in which the beans lay – hard and unrelenting, they had boiled and bubbled right through lunch and dinner before acquiring an edible softness.

Marina blamed the kitchen's electric hobs for her culinary misfortunes. They released a tepid and tentative heat, while she needed the steady, azure flames of a gas connection for her chickpeas, black-eyed peas, butter beans and other tough legumes. She also blamed herself for arriving at the university without a pressure cooker – the kind that whistled to announce that a legume or a portion of meat had grown tender and worthy of being marinated or put into a curry.

She decided to thwart her longings for the flavours of a Bahia street, and cook only the kind of food that required little heat or inventiveness. Pastas of all varieties yielded readily to the slow warmth of the hob, and she convinced herself that her daily experiments with fusilli or vermicelli or ribbon-cut lasagne were a part of a process of internationalisation that had begun – as promised by the university's orientation handout – the moment she had landed here with her canary yellow suitcase.

Marina's internationalisation, despite being slow and painful like the hob she was slouched over, led her to scour the internet for recipes. It was important for a variety of reasons, to prepare the fusilli with its subtle sauce of fresh avocados – halved, pitted and mashed – with the effortlessness of a new cosmopolite. The dish would be a fragrant confirmation of her cross-border cookery skills. It would also give the impression of silent efficiency and composure to Xiuying, who, in spite of her outburst, was cooking with an instinctive ability to turn raw food into gastronomic delights.

Marina cut a cup full of cherry tomatoes into soft halves as the fusilli and Xiuying boiled on steadily. She sprinkled some olive oil on the tomatoes and added basil leaves to the pulpy mix. She nodded vigorously when Xiuying said something about Kevin being a pig, and wondered if trying to placate her spurned flatmate while making the best avocado sauce in Norwich would delay her for her biodiversity audit. Later in the day, she would study the molecular structure of plankton under a microscope – a task she found easier to perform than beating avocado pulp to a smooth consistency. She whisked some of the pasta water into the mashed avocado, and added the juice of a plump lemon to the sauce. She tasted it by poking her index finger into the bowl and placing a twirl of sauce on the tip of her tongue – a movement both swift and defiant, for it distracted Xiuying enough to stop her tirade for a few seconds and frown disapprovingly at the blasphemy of a microbe-riddled finger touching food meant for human consumption.

The sauce was 'bursting with flavour' just as the recipe had reassuringly stated. Marina stirred the pasta and the mixture of cherry tomatoes into it. Her lunch was ready, but Xiuying, she could tell, was in the mood for conversation. Did she just ask her a question? Was it rhetorical? Marina decided on a quick and corny reply, which she blurted out with what she hoped was the élan and wisdom of a Hispanic agony aunt. She opened the kitchen door to leave, and nearly bumped into Kethaki Gupta who occupied Flat 2D. She exchanged a quick smile with the gregarious Indian girl and walked out with her pasta, relieved that Xiuying would have someone else to talk to as she ate a meal that reminded her of a love affair in its heyday.

Did plankton have feelings, Marina wondered, as she ate her pasta in her room and heard Xiuying sob in the kitchen, probably into her meticulously prepared pig kidneys.

Scrambled Eggs on (Unburnt) Toast

'Oh Xiuying, what's the big deal? A break-up is not something you sit and cry about; it's something you sing about or dance about.' Kethaki Gupta disseminated wisdom as she cracked open the reddish-brown shells of two medium-sized eggs, the produce of well-bred Suffolk hens. The yolks fell into a deep ceramic bowl and Kethaki whipped them with her balloon-bottomed whisk. She stopped her rhythmic thak-thak-thak every now and then, to say something profound to Xiuying, who was sniffling softly as she forked the food on her plate.

'Bollywood has a million song-and-dance sequences dedicated to break-ups,' Kethaki continued, adding a pinch of salt and half a teaspoon of freshly-ground pepper to her whisked eggs. 'So if you are *really* feeling that terrible, why not put your arms around a silver oak on campus and sing to it,' she advised, placing a frying pan on the hob and dropping a splotch of butter into it.

Kethaki's homilies were like the food she cooked – absurdly simple and nourishing to the spirit. On most days, she tore open a plastic carton of Sainsbury's *Tarka Dal – Earthy and Aromatic* – and heated it in the microwave. She then ate the dal with a garlic and coriander naan or with some rice that had boiled and bubbled in her rice cooker – a stout and overworked vessel that had travelled all the way from India with her. But on days that she decided to cook, her 'cooking-shooking days', she would simply add a fistful of mung dal to the rice and sprinkle some salt and turmeric into the cooker. She would allow the concoction, a khichri, to jiggle away in the cooker, till it had softened enough to eat.

'Khichri is great if you want a belly that doesn't jingle-jangle when you walk,' she would say to her flatmates, shovelling mouthfuls of the yellowy mess into her mouth, as they laboured over their meals.

Kethaki's culinary talents extended to eggs – fried, scrambled and the Indian variants, masala omelette and tomato bhurji. And now, as she poured the beaten eggs into the pan with its glaze of melted butter, she noticed that Xiuying was smiling. Finally. The eggs curdled and she shovelled with a wooden ladle to prevent the foamy mix from sticking to the frying pan.

'Be a bit like Meena Kumari, Xiuying. Sing your heart out to a bottle of Merlot,' she said, as she removed the frying pan from the hob and transferred the soft, moist scrambled eggs onto a plate.

'Who is Meena Kum... oh look, there's smoke coming out of the toaster!' Xiuying said suddenly, nearly screaming the second half of her sentence. The thought of food being rendered inedible due to human stupidity was unbearable to her.

Kethaki had forgotten about the slices of sunflower-seed bread she had put into the toaster. They were burnt to a crisp, but she was unfazed.

'Never mind. I'll just fry some rice and put the eggs in it. I'll have scrambled-eggs-fried-rice for lunch today,' she said calmly.

'Add some soy sauce,' Xiuying replied.

Soy sauce. A few drops could make both lunch and life tolerable, at least for the moment.

Radhika Oberoi grew up in India and has moonlighted as a journalist for the *Times of India*, the *Hindu Literary Review* and, more recently, the *New York Times* blog, *India Ink*. Her day job required her to sit at a desk and work in an advertising firm.

ANNA POOK

Bigger, Brighter Things

Novel extract.

Prologue

WHOEVER DESIGNED MY PE KIT IS A SADIST: STIFF, BLACK SHORTS that ride up my thighs and a scratchy polo shirt that bobbles after each wash, and hisses with static as Mum shakes it free from the washing machine. The worst thing, though, is the colour. Amber, the egg-yolk yellow of flickering indecision, the moment between stop and go. No wonder we're all crap at PE; we are walking metaphors, traffic lights stuck in limbo, waiting aimlessly in muddy fields for the green light of adulthood.

I get halfway to school before I realise I've left my kit in a crumpled heap on the hallway floor. I could lie and tell Miss Little I've got my period, but if her maths is anything as good as her shot put, she'll know it's not possible to have a period for three weeks running. Unwilling to risk the wrath of my least favourite teacher, I press the bell and wait for the bus to stop so I can trudge the mile-and-a-half home in the spitting rain.

As I cross Norwood High Street I contemplate the chances of a four foot eleven woman being called Miss Little. Maybe it's one of God's pastimes, creating his own set of Mister Men down here on Earth. Doesn't he have better things to do?

By the time I get to the front door, I've renamed each one of my teachers. Now there's a knack to opening our front door. You have to push the key to the left before turning it clockwise in the lock, pulling the door towards you a bit, then shoving it with your shoulder. But it won't budge.

'Hello. Is anyone there?' I shout through the letterbox.

Josh is probably at school by now, and Mum's at work. I don't want to walk to the phone box and spend my tuck shop money on a call because Dad can't rouse himself from his lie-in. I've saved just enough change for a Toffee Crisp.

'Dad, are you in there? Dad. Open up.' I press the doorbell extra hard as if it will increase the volume.

No answer.

Through the letterbox I can see the kitchen door at the end of the hallway is closed. I scan the floor looking for my kit, squinting into the darkness. And that's when I see him, lying on his back, only metres away from me. My eyes seek the things that make sense, the rolled-up sleeves of his shirt, the glint of his belt buckle, and the thick soles of his shoes. And then they rest on the dark red patch blossoming on his chest, the blood on his hands, the floor, the walls.

I push all my weight against the door but it's no use. Dad has bolted it shut from the inside.

1.
Four Months Ago

I don't want to go to school on the first day back, I want to stay at home with Dad and watch repeats of *Give Us a Clue* in my pyjamas. No matter how famous you are, no matter how beautiful, you can't play charades without looking like a moron. It's a leveller, the opposite of school, which has more layers than Mum's trifle. To rise to the top, you need a Naf Naf bomber jacket and a fit boyfriend. It doesn't take much to sink to the bottom.

Dad has settled himself on his side of the sofa as I'm leaving, his pale legs propped up on the coffee table, a move he only dares make once Mum has left the house. His dressing gown is getting too small and hangs loose at his sides – too many mornings in front of the telly with nothing better to do than dip Rich Tea biscuits into his coffee, testing how long he can dunk before the biscuit disintegrates.

I hold up my hand to him.

'Five words,' he says.

'I'm saying bye, Dad.'

'Oh right, of course,' he says, his beard full of crumbs. 'See you tonight. Usual spot, all right love?'

Whenever Dad collects me he parks round the corner from the school gates, incognito. Sometimes he takes it too far, covering his face with a copy of the *Daily Mirror*.

'You'd better go or you'll be late,' he says.

I touch my nose with my right index finger and point to him with the other hand, charades-speak for, 'Spot on.'

Our form room is a time warp. As soon as I step inside, the whole summer disappears. It's like I've never been away from the science block, its scratched wooden desks and dying house plants.

Miss Gottlieb, my form tutor, is writing her quote of the day onto the blackboard, stopping every couple of letters to wipe her glasses clean with her fingers:

'And now we welcome the new (school) year. Full of things that have never been.'

Rilke

The boy sitting in my seat has never been here before. He's wearing a bomber jacket = good, that is torn at the elbow and splashed with paint = bad, and drawing on the back of his hand in blue biro.

'You're in my seat,' I say, drumming my fingers on the desk.

He doesn't flinch, just adds a leg to the panther taking shape on his tanned skin. A tiny freckle has been circled to make an eye.

My second tactic – coughing – only succeeds in gaining Miss Gottlieb's attention; the impostor doesn't take his eyes off his artistry.

'Is there a problem, Genevieve?'

I point to my chair. I'm Baby Bear staring forlornly at his occupied bed.

'Neil is new to this class so I suggested he sit near the front,' she says. 'Go and sit next to Luke.'

Great. Luke is the class clown or, more accurately, the class loudmouth. People leave him alone for one reason: his ogre of a dad is head of the Science Department. If we mess with Luke, Mr Ellis gets happy with a Bunsen burner.

I slouch over to my new seat, dragging my platform heels along the worn-out parquet. There is some comfort in knowing this path has been trodden by hundreds of people before me, former pupils that survived the experience and went on to bigger, brighter things. One day the marks I make will be all that remains of my time here.

'All right darling?' says Luke, flicking his tongue in and out and winking at me in a way he considers suggestive.

'I can see you,' says Miss Gottlieb with her back to us, tapping the wing mirror she's gaffer-taped to the side of the blackboard. We all know what prompted it. Last term, someone stole her plastic anatomy model, Penelope, from right under her nose. Poor 'Penny' showed up on the sports field, disembowelled.

'Right everyone,' says Miss Gottlieb, perching on the edge of her desk. 'One privilege of entering Year 12 is the chance to represent your fellow classmates in the school collegium.'

'The *what?*' says Luke, his nose scrunching up in disgust.

'The COLL–E–GI–UM,' says Miss Gottlieb, stretching out each syllable, enunciating but failing to explain.

'The school government,' I whisper in his ear.

'Government!' says Luke. 'Why would anyone want to be a part of that sleazy bunch of losers?'

Miss Gottlieb blushes, turns to Neil, who still hasn't looked up from his drawing.

'I don't think all of them are like that. Some politicians are worthy, generous-hearted individuals who put the needs of the community first.'

'I'm going to report this to the headmaster,' says Luke. 'Someone's kidnapped Miss Gottlieb and replaced her with a party political broadcast.'

'Yes, thank you Luke, very good. But how would you feel if I said all school children were indolent layabouts with nothing between the ears?'

I want to touch my nose with my right index finger and point at Miss Gottlieb with the other hand. From the look on his face, Luke's searching the recesses of his brain for the definition of indolent.

'I'm not asking you to march into Downing Street,' says Miss Gottlieb. 'I'm asking you to take part in the school council, to use your voice to make a difference, to improve the experience of each and every one of the two thousand students at this school.'

I know where you could start, I think: add a Tampax machine to the girls' toilets, ban the hundred metre hurdles for all time and take turkey burgers off the lunch menu.

'You have ten minutes to get into pairs and prepare your speeches. Here are some questions to help you get started.' She distributes pink A4 sheets she's gone to the trouble of laminating. 'When the time is up, you are going to put your partner forward as collegium candidate.'

'What if we don't want to stand?' It's Neil. He's finally deemed us worthy of his attention. I was beginning to think he was mute.

'Why? Got a problem with your legs?' shouts Luke.

Neil turns and I see his face for the first time. One of his eyes is green, the other hazel. Depending on which eye I focus on, his face completely changes. Both looks are disarmingly beautiful, even when he's angry.

'I meant stand for election, you idiot.'

The whole class goes silent but I know exactly what they're thinking: *Fee! Fi! Fo! Fum*! I smell the singed hair of the mouthy one. Someone should have prepped Neil; he walked into that completely blind.

'Candidature for the collegium is not compulsory but everyone is required to participate in today's class, including you.'

We've got an odd number of people in class so Miss Gottlieb volunteers to partner up with Luke and I'm with Neil.

When he looks at me it's like he's staring straight through me. I even turn around to check he's not actually eyeing Penelope, who's propped up on the shelf behind me, her blood-red mess of a heart on display.

'OK,' he says. 'Let's start with you.'

Anna Pook is currently working on her debut novel *Things Can Only Get Better*, a bittersweet social comedy set in 1997. She is the 2014/15 recipient of the UEA Booker Scholarship.

MARIE-ELSA ROCHE

The Juniper Tree

Extract from a novel.

THE LAKE WAS ALWAYS A SURPRISE. THE EDGES WERE HIS. HE COULD cut their shape into the ground with a knife, but the water made him stare. Grey-blue eyes sinking in to find something. For a while it was still. Mountains bowed deep into its bed. Hemp sat with him, mouth slightly open, his head flicking occasionally to one side of the lake, and the other. Then the sun lit up the banks. It yellowed the grass. His mother would be baking, he thought, or maybe Catherine will be up and folding sweet, creamy mixture into her black trays, her buckled hands clasping the spoon. He wondered what the hall felt like without him or his father there.

His bag was tightly packed with packets of soup, tins of corned beef and sardines, but he pulled out a tub of cake, vanilla sponge with gooseberry jam. The taste seemed perfumed compared to the stillness of the view. He watched and slowly felt a lump in his chest and then pressure in his head before tears. He could hear the radio, listening to the races back by the hearth in the farm; him and his father with a bet on. He saw the paperwork on the table, a mug of tea, the checked notebooks of annual bills and his school books, pages of homework done, his football cards sorted by the window: Moore, Charlton, Wilkins. He watched and the length of time felt weary.

He fed Hemp, rubbing the dog's belly under his long white fur, and checked his blue eye again for leadening. And after some milk chocolate, he set off along the water's edge and into the wood. Sheer streaks of slate cracked into the lake. His headache made his eyelid flicker. On the far side, he moved past the rushes and mallow ponds and through

McKenzie's field, but soon became aware of Hemp growling. 'It'll be one lambing,' he said, as if his father was near, racing back together. And the ewe was on her side, belly swelling in and out like bellows to a fire. He knelt near, not wanting to scare her, and watched as the milky sack ballooned out and muddied. He could just see the lamb, the beginning of a white face, black eyes and dots of hooves, the sack swaying. Hemp was on the other side, lying low.

'Ye daft mottle. Git ere.'

He held his arm open for the dog to curl in and watch. But the sheep saw Hemp move and tried to bolt, scrambling to stand, heaving belly falling back onto the head, bursting the sac. Stephen lurched forward, grabbing the sheep and pressed her to the ground, cutting his thigh on a stone, leaning his knee on her leg, his hand on her head to stop her jolting, to free her belly.

'Down now, down.'

The sheep looked at him from the side with a wide, maddened eye and Stephen jerked with shock. His belly stung and he roared. The sound scared him, he felt pain in his joints and his gut. He spat and burst, straining to hold it in, pressing on the sheep's neck and roared again. It filled the space across the lake. Hemp began to bark and Stephen saw his father on the ledge of Wandope, curled for the night, cold. He remembered his father's eye, wide to the side and the way he didn't know him, the sounds he made, reluctant to be moved. No words, just sounds of disgust. And then, as he pulled his father's arm around his neck and tried to help him up, the heavy weight of his broad body slumping down, falling loose.

'Come on, Dad. We'll be having you home.'

But his father just wept, slapping his outspread legs with his knuckles, hands clenched with the pain, head falling forward.

'Dad, it's me, Stephen. It'll be all right now. We just need to get you home. We've all been out looking for you again. You've been up here in the fells into the night, Dad. Come on now.' But his father knelt, head in his hands and shook sobbing to the ground, to the muddy shingles, leaning his head onto them. And then he began to bang, forehead thudding into the slate.

'Ey, no, now Dad. Not that, no,' Stephen called as he struggled with his father's broad shoulders, trying to pull him up, but the hitting got stronger and the murmurs of sobs became a rage and he roared. And then he roared again, and again as if he were vomiting sound until he pushed and Stephen swung back to find his father up and facing him, bloodied brow dripping, shouting, ready to flatten him.

'Away, ya devil! Awe'eth ya! I see thou. Away!' Staring from under his bunched brow, breathing heavily through his dripping nostrils like a bull.

'Dad, it's me.'

'Away, no, away now.' He staggered, blinking to the ground, fists poised for battle, his head wet. Stephen stepped back, choking tears.

'Please Dad, come home.'

'No, I'll not go home, no place for me,' he swayed. 'I'm not beaten yet.'

'Please let me help,' Stephen cried and the old man looked up to his son, wild, but recognising something of him for a moment.

'No, lad. It'll be in these fells or not at all.'

'But Dad, you'll be all right, just come home.'

'Get yourself away now, or I'll thrash yer!' He said, fists clenched, body shaking and he tumbled towards Stephen. 'I mean it! I'll thrash yer! Get away! Get away!' And Stephen ran, vision blurred, teared, to get help, leaving his father on the ledge, overhanging the sheer slate scree, heavy with night.

Breathless, Stephen focused on the edge of the lake, the grass and then the sheep. 'Come on now!' he called with tears and let his heavy head fall forward while he reached over and slipped his hand around and under the back of the lamb's head to pull it out, the sticky sack covering his skin, warm water down his arm. He pulled, mindful of the suction, and the sheep kicked while the lamb's head slid out and rested, complete in itself, white and asleep. Then its body: yellow wool swaddled in glutinous white.

Thighs holding the sheep, Stephen scraped his finger into the lamb's mouth, scrubbed its nostrils with grass and gathered it into both hands, bringing its limp body, in as much sac as possible, over to the mother's face. He stayed close, lying behind her, holding her in, his chest on her back, his blood blotting her wool, carefully bending her towards the lamb, to the smell.

'Come on, mother,' he whispered gently. 'Come on there now,' and he held her till he felt her licking, while the twists of umbilical chord slithered out with the placenta and, as she licked, he gently rolled away, leaving them together. The lamb waking, shuddering its head, soon splaying its hooves, ready to stand and then to feed, darting at the underbelly, tail wiggling.

Over the far side of Crummock Lake, Stephen refused the presence of Red Pike, pushing the purple grey away, as if there were lakes on either side of him. When he got to Lingcombe Edge the light changed and he quickened towards Melbreak valley as it opened in front, sun deepening the green of grass here and there, lighting the side of a tree.

By early evening the clouds parted fully in the nook between the twin fells, Lingcombe and Melbreak, and veins of rusted yellow slowly climbed down the valley at their own pace. Stephen's camp was set under the tall juniper, a silver birch partly entwined. A good place to rest, he thought. He threw a large stick into the lake and watched Hemp's white nose and black ears bob after it. His arm was cramping so he moved around, taking in the stringent air, and then walked the valley, luscious in its meadow mint, dandelions, forget-me-nots and speedwells; their colours pulling him this way and that, catching the sun.

As he ate, the light threaded into blood amber until twilight thinned the air and then, for a moment, a breathless silence drew his sight to the distance where dark streaks pulled over the lake: rain making a stake in the ground. It came in fast, hissing at the waters, stinging the waves to break in on each other. He made a cover with some tarpaulin under the branches of the juniper tree and pulled Hemp by his collar onto his lap, his long fur soaked. The sky cracked, thunder raced on the ground and thick, purple clouds hammered.

He must have slept wet that night. The following morning the lake was white. Mist so still, it absorbed him and the valley. The haze thickened to pearl before light came from behind Robinson, steaming, unwrapping the mountains. His body was numb with cold and as the sun rested on him he warmed and felt his father there. Remembered the feeling as they leant against the tree, the weight of him. Tenderness pressed on him and burrowed into his heart like a fist, knuckles twisting, and the dust around him lifted in the heat like smoke from fire, incense into clear skies. He leant out towards the lake and reached, hovering, fragile over the waters. Sadness seeped out of him like spring rain, lilting in the light. Colours lit from the dust rising.

That afternoon as he walked, he cleared the grasses of last year's twigs and old wood. He pulled out bracken, bent and frayed, black rotten roots, dragging the gnarled branches left to moss and crumble. He wasn't sure why he gathered old lint, just bent and clawed the reeds, tugging gorse with prickled hands, buttercup pollen on his sleeves, freeing thorned bushel. He worked till the sun blazed its final red once again, and he kept working as lines of puce pinched into dusk-ochre and faded with the taste of lemon. The mountains still neon, backlit, like peering through a door.

As darkness settled and the chill of clear sky pricked his skin, he lit the mound of fire blazing into the night. Silt and smoke raced in tar black. Sap spat and tinder sparks snapped, hot tendered, stoked through the early hours till the fire's embers joined with the dawn. And there, covered in ash, he felt worn and heavy enough to sleep. Kneeling, pink eyed, a quick glance up to the nook between the twin fells, and he saw something moving, a man, maybe someone he knew. Too bright at first, but in time it was clearer; a stranger walking down through the valley towards him, the spring of cowslip, yarrow and heather beneath his feet. Meadowsweet morning seeping through the grasses, lifting their heads, marrying cotton-soft smoke. Stephen was so tired he could hardly watch.

Marie-Elsa Roche is half-French, half-Cumbrian. She read philosophy and theology at Oxford and has been an Anglican priest for ten years. She is working on *The Juniper Tree*.

GRAHAM RUSHE

When You Look
Across the River

H E SITS THERE LOOKING ACROSS THE RIVER, WAITING FOR HER TO arrive. In the top pocket of the old army jacket he's wearing are two joints that he's just finished rolling. The sun belts down, slapping the back of his neck.

She's late – they were supposed to meet at half past four, but it's almost hitting ten to five. He stamps the ground nervously with his worn DC runners. Hearing the hedge rustle behind him, he turns his head and sees Anna making her way into the open, walking down the bank towards him. She stops when she reaches the clearing. They've spent so much of their leaving cert year down here that a perimeter of the grass has died out.

'How's it going?' he says, cupping a hand over his eyes to get a good look at her.

Even dressed in her school uniform he thinks she's dead stunning, has always thought so, and has carried it with him like a chain, not wanting the other lads to know, as they'd only abuse him.

She gazes across the river before sitting down beside him. 'I'm all right, and yourself Joseph?'

'Grand, sure the usual,' he says taking a joint out of his pocket. He likes that she calls him Joseph and not Joe, which is what everybody else calls him. 'How was school today?' he asks, lighting the spliff.

'Same old, same old. You?'

'Myself and Kevin mitched double French, shot a few frames up in Mickey's.'

'Nothing new there huh,' she says. 'You'd want to start putting in a few hours, the exams aren't too far away now.'

Joseph's aware French and maths are going down the pan. He often visualises the moment his auld pair see his results. The mother will probably bawl and his father will look like he's got a stick shoved up his arse. More than likely, they'll plead with him to repeat, but no fuckin' chance is he doing that craic. He isn't a dunce: he just hasn't done a tap all year.

'I'm thinking of dropping down to pass French anyways,' he says.

She doesn't respond. Usually she'd chastise him for having such a defeatist outlook, but today she's staring off into the distance, preoccupied by something, he reckons. She must be thinking about Paddy's Day. Fuck that was almost two months ago now. They haven't been talking properly since.

'It's an awful pity about young Brian,' she says, digging her fingers into the dirt.

He takes a deep inhale and feels the smoke swirl around his chest. Looking at the river, Joseph notices the lazy pull of the water as some reeds drift slowly by. 'It's an awful tragedy. My mother hasn't shut up about it since it happened like.'

Joseph was shocked when his mother told him about it: a seven-year-old boy drowning right across from the spot where he always hangs out.

Young Brian apparently kicked a football over the back wall of his house, followed it down to where it lay in the water, close to the bank. Stretching for it, on his knees, young Brian lost his balance and fell into the river. Well, that's what the rumours say happened.

Joseph hasn't slept well since the accident. Things in the social group are slightly strained because of him, and if they weren't then maybe his gang would've been here when Brian kicked the ball over, been here to save his life.

To deal with the guilt he's smoking more hash than usual.

'That's his place over there.' Joseph points to the back of a semi-detached house, less than a hundred metres away.

'The family must be heartbroken,' she says, as he nudges her to take the joint off him.

Anna looks at him hesitantly.

'Ah go on, you're not going to let me smoke all this to myself. I'll be baked as fuck.'

She smiles at him nervously and shakes her head.

'Really, not like you to say no to a smoke,' he says, feeling like a bit of an idiot.

A silence hangs over them as they sit side by side, not looking at each other.

Again, he starts patting the ground with his feet. It's apparent to him that things are still awkward, have been for almost a couple of months now since the night they shagged on the other side of the river, which was pretty close to the spot the boy drowned. Some of the police tape is still wrapped around the bark of one of the trees.

They'd been knacker drinking there, a bunch of them, on Paddy's Day. It was the first time he'd taken pills and he remembered telling Anna how he loved her, always had. The magic thing was that she started kissing him. They made their way through the trees, sat down close to the water, chatted about everything and everyone. While it was still pitch black out and when the sounds of the rest of the gang had waned, almost to a murmur, they had sex.

The next morning Joseph woke up in his bed feeling like a pig shat in his head, but at the same time, a euphoria swept over him. Everything had led to this. He texted Anna straight away and said to himself that he would not stir from the bed until she replied. He was pure giddy.

It took her almost a fortnight to text him back. In his stupidity he'd told his best friend Bob not to tell anybody that he'd popped his cherry, shagged Anna. Everybody in school knew a few days later. She resented him for it, he knew that, had to hear it off of her friends. The greatest moment of Joseph's life quickly became his most despised.

The wind picks up slightly, bristling through Joseph's hair. 'Want to hang out tomorrow, grab lunch, the two of us?' he asks, hearing his heartbeat quicken, he's never asked her out properly like this before.

She pauses. 'I would… but I'm actually going over to Liverpool with my mother for a few days.'

'Really? You visiting family?'

'No, the two of us are just going to do a bit of shopping like,' she says, taking her phone out of her pocket and inspecting it.

'Isn't it well for some,' he says, taking a large inhale from the spliff. Anna doesn't reply. Something's between them now, he knows it, can sense it cutting the air. She keeps glancing across the water, away from him. He feels like a muppet for picking this place to meet her; he's only done it to try and prove things can be normal again between them. The tragedy of young Brian should've been enough for him to realise that this place is now tainted.

The silence breaks with the sound of her sobbing.

'Anna, are you all right? What's the matter?'

She leans over, wraps her arms around him, plants her head in his chest. 'The child.'

'I know, it's awful to think that something like that can happen in this day and age.' It's not enough. He has to say something philosophical, all encompassing, that will put her at ease and make her realise that he's the man she needs to be with. Holding her tightly, he wants to smell her hair, but thinks it an inappropriate time.

'It's a tragedy,' is all he can say, over and over again.

After several minutes, she loosens her grip, pulls away from him. 'I've got to go. I'll see you soon,' she says, standing up, wiping her face.

He stands up too. 'Are you sure you're all right...' The words get caught in his mouth, like they always do in crucial moments like this. He wants to put his arms around her again, comfort her, but she's moved away, is retreating now. This moment feels crucial to him and he's letting it slip away.

'I'll catch you soon,' she says. With that she turns around, walks back up the slope.

'Enjoy the holiday!' he shouts after her, but she doesn't acknowledge him.

Today is the day he'd planned to turn it all around and he'd made an arse of it. He strolls to the riverbank and starts skimming stones. Soon his mother will have the tea on the table.

Late that night, with the air all dewy, Joseph makes his way behind the row of houses, through the hedges, back to the river. He has to use the light on his phone to help him find the way and his shoes are sopping as he wades through all the wild uncut grass to the familiar clearing. The dirt is OK to sit on, not too wet, and leaning back he sparks up the joint that he never smoked earlier. It'd been a shit day, shit evening and shit night. He dropped all the other fellas 'cause he thought he'd a shot of spending the evening with Anna. No doubt the boys were wrecked at this stage, probably in the beer garden of The Brig, drinking naggins they smuggled in. Joseph could have joined them, but is too deflated. The clouds are out in force and he can barely make out any of the stars above him.

What will he do after school? After the results come through he'll be able to sign on officially. Anna will be off to one of the cities: Galway, Cork, even Limerick. She'd get the points no bother; she'd brains on her. They'd all be together for the next few months and then there'd be a split between those who left and the ones who stayed. Sure the majority would come back at weekends to hit up The Brig, but it wouldn't be the same. He's not fully sure how he knows this, but he does, feels it deep inside of him, almost as distinctly as the hash running through his system.

He stubs the joint out, flicks it down the slope. Lifting his head up, he rubs his chin, inspects the opposite side of the river. Nothing can be heard except the low sweeping sound of the water brushing by.

That's when he sees it: a child standing amongst the reeds across on the far bank. Joseph leans forward, his hands pressed down on the dirt. Focusing as hard as he can, he expects this mirage to disappear any second. His heart is beating violently. Jesus H Christ, this must be some sort of super skunk.

'Hello, are you all right?' Joseph shouts.

The figure doesn't budge, doesn't mutter a syllable.

This has to be young Brian; this must be his ghost. The sweat is dripping down Joseph's forehead fast now. 'Is it you, Brian?' he shouts over.

He stands up, takes a few steps forward. A beam of moonlight breaks through some of the cloud cover and he catches a clear look of the pale, dark-haired child that's staring at him across the water. Young Brian was a ginger, where this child has a mop of dark hair like his own.

Moving closer, he almost falls over a rock.

'You don't even know who I am.'

Joseph stops in his tracks, looks around him. There is nobody in sight. The voice was as clear as day; he couldn't have imagined it.

The child is still looking at him and a shiver runs up his spine. Every fibre of his being is telling him to scatter till he's back in his bedroom with the door fastened shut.

'What do you want?' Joseph asks. 'Are you real?'

He gets no response, but the child keeps staring at him, and he can't avert his gaze either.

Joseph walks forward to the edge of the river.

Taking off his shoes and coat, he smiles at the child, and breathing heavily, he leaps into the water, begins thrashing to the other side. Clawing his way onto the bank, he notices the child is gone.

Graham Rushe is from County Clare, Ireland. He studied English and Scottish Literature at the University of Aberdeen. Upon graduating in 2014 he won the university's annual creative writing award: The Bobby Aitken Memorial Prize. He is currently working on a novel, provisionally titled *How to Forget*.

Under the Tiger's Eye

Extract from a novel.

B Y ELEVEN ANITA WAS DRUNK. SHE'D HAD THREE SCREWDRIVERS ON an empty stomach and danced far too much. Her friends continued on the dancefloor as she returned to the table. Out of the corner of her eye she saw Avinash make a beeline towards her.

'Hey,' she said, sitting down on one of the cold plastic chairs.

'Hey,' he said, joining her, raising a near-empty glass. 'Get you another drink?'

'I don't think that's such a good idea.'

'Oh, come on, Anita, one drink. This is your last big night out, isn't it?' He smirked. 'Might as well party properly, no?'

'Not right now. Where's Bharat?'

'Why? I'm sure your baby brother can manage just fine without you.'

She frowned.

'I saw him push off with the boys back to the parking lot for another joint.'

'Fool,' she said without malice. It was one thing returning home smelling of alcohol and smoke, it was another returning home with pink eyes. He needed to be careful, otherwise Uma Aunty would give them both a proper thrashing.

Avinash downed his drink, looked around, and then asked, 'How about we see the tiger now?'

'Now?' She inspected his expression. 'I thought you said the place was closed.'

'That doesn't mean we can't go there.'

'You want to go now?'

'Why not?' He raised an eyebrow.

It was unfair to see it without Bharat, but then again, he would have more opportunities in the future to do so than she would. Her reckless voice egged her on. This was her last chance before the States. 'OK. You're sure it's no problem, right?'

He was already up, face shining with enthusiasm. 'Let's go, let's go,' he said, clapping his hands like a drill instructor.

She stood up, swayed, and he leaned forward and supported her, one arm gliding down to her lower back. They walked out to the lawn, past the swimming pool – its shifting surface reflecting shards of yellow light – towards one of the larger blue-and-white painted buildings with a circular driveway and steps that led to a columned entrance.

There was no one around. Anita, halfway up the stairs, took off her heels and carried them by her fingertips. They strode past the entrance into the muffled silence of a wide foyer. The smell of ink and oil hung thick in the air, and on the walls were green bulletin boards with pinned-up typewritten sheets of member by-laws. Potted plants and worn leather couches lined the sides of the room. From the ceiling descended a glass chandelier, ornate, glittering, the bulbs for candles empty and waiting. Anita's feet were cold on the white marble floor.

Avinash held a hand up, motioned for her to wait, and took a few tentative steps, peering down one of the hallways before beckoning her forward. She followed. They walked down a narrow and dimly lit hallway with high walls. There were gold-framed photographs of British soldiers resting, of members decked in suits, posing with cigars in one hand and a drink in the other, of a huntsman standing with his kill, gun on his shoulder. Looking up, she could see the stuffed heads of stags and bison, their silhouettes sharp despite the dark. And then, at the end of the corridor, on the floor, were rainbow-coloured fragments of light cast by glass and she knew, knew with such certainty that she gasped, that the tiger was there, waiting for her after all those years.

They rounded the corner and on display was the glass case containing the mythical animal. The glass was not clean, faded around the corners, but as she stepped closer, Anita could make out the shape of the tiger, its astonishingly large size, and then the colours began to fill in the space, slices of black cutting rich orange, making it whole, bringing with it a brilliance she could not have even imagined. Oh, if only Bharat was there. They should have seen it together.

Anita knelt and pressed her face to the glass. Just as she had heard from her friends, the tiger was poised to attack, the front of its body low, the thighs tensed. Its claws were extended, cruelly curved. Nestled within blades of yellow teeth was a faded pink tongue. She was shocked to see a bald patch on one leg, fur on the tail that had faded to resemble wisps of straw. It was heartbreaking. The more she looked, the more it seemed the skin of the animal didn't fit as naturally as it should, as though there was something within straining to get out. One eye was missing, but the other, though made of glass, was alive; glinted green in the dark, moved with her, watched her, anticipating her every move.

'What do you think?' Avinash asked.

She stood up, felt a rush of blood to her head that made her dizzy, and tottered towards him. 'It's brilliant. Sad, but brilliant.'

'Uh huh,' he said, his voice shades deeper, and then his hand cupped her chin and he kissed her.

Anita, startled, felt his intrusive tongue slide into her mouth before she pulled back and sputtered, 'Oh, sorry. Sorry, no, I wasn't expecting that.'

'It's OK,' he said, stretching the final vowel out as he leaned forward.

Anita pulled back. 'No. Sorry,' she repeated, abashed but annoyed she was apologising so much.

'No problem.' He strained a smile.

Anita looked around and then said, 'Come on, shall we go? I really need to use the loo anyway.'

He nodded and pointed. Right across from where they stood was the doorway to the women's bathroom. She excused herself and stepped inside. The bathroom was plush. Gleaming white tiles and black marble counters. Even the porcelain sinks were spotless. She placed her shoes on the counter as the bathroom door opened and Avinash stepped inside. His reflection's eyes met hers.

She turned. 'Women's bathroom,' she said as a joke, even though her heart was already beating hard. There was a thin vein that split his forehead in two, and he glanced behind him before letting the door shut. 'Avinash, seriously,' she whispered, voice catching. Her high was gone, replaced by a clammy sensation weakening her legs.

Avinash smiled and raised his hands, as though to indicate he had no secrets up his sleeves. 'What's the big deal? I was just checking to make sure you were OK.' He took a step forward and there radiated from his body a smell, not unpleasant, of coconut oil. 'Come on, Anita,' he said. 'You're smashed. I'm just trying to help.'

He was too close to her now, and all Anita could think were the feeble words, 'Women's bathroom,' dying on her lips. His hands were on her arms. Anita stiffened and pulled her face away from him.

His face tightened. 'What's wrong? What's the big deal?'

Bitter fumes of alcohol mingled with the smell of coconut. 'Avinash, stop.' She needed to defuse the situation, to make him realise. 'Please stop. I just want to go, do you understand?'

'It'll be fun, Anita, come on.' He leaned his body into her, so that their faces were inches apart, and then Anita felt his hardness against her thigh, just as he grabbed her hand and plunged it inside his trousers. She yanked her arm away, tried to pull her entire body free, but he wrestled with her, rammed her against the sink counter and pressed himself against her. He was panting. He bent down and bit into her neck, sucked flesh.

Anita grunted in repulsion and shoved. He fell backwards onto the floor, his trousers undone, his erection straining against the fabric. She leapt for the door, swung it open, just as he grabbed her ankle and pulled her down. She fell, her knees squeaking against white marble, half her body out the bathroom. There, under the tiger's eye, Avinash climbed on top of Anita, grabbed both of her wrists with one hand and pinned them to her chest, while with his other hand he hitched her dress up and fumbled with her underwear.

There was no more restraint; Anita lashed out. She kicked hard, again and again, her feet pounding wall. She contorted her torso, writhing as she bucked his heavy body, trying to dislodge the sharp knee in her stomach. 'Stop, stop,' he kept saying, shushing her, and then suddenly his fingers roughly thrust themselves inside her, splitting her as they scraped her insides. A screen of red obscured Anita's vision. She was screaming, spitting, thrashing under the weight of his body. 'Stop,' he commanded, shoving his fingers deeper insider her, widening her. He looked down, at where their groins and his hand met, and Anita looked too, could see the head of his penis, purple, throbbing, poking out of his trousers' zippers. 'No,' she gasped, and then she craned her neck, reached with all her might, and bit deep into his forearm, tearing skin from flesh.

He yelped and rolled off her. 'For fuck's sake, Anita!'

But she was already up, running, as hard as she could, away from him, from the glass case, from the eyes in the photographs on the wall, from the eyes in the dead animals above. Anita ran straight into a steward.

It was the same one who had checked their passes, and he frowned at her. 'Madam? Everything OK? Did you just now shout?'

She gasped for air, pointing behind her, unsure whether Avinash would casually appear, adjusting his cuffs with a smile on his face.

The steward understood. 'Stay here, Madam.' He walked past her, disappearing down the corridor. It was silent in the hall, the air thick around Anita. She trembled. Her wrists were sore from where Avinash had held her and there was a scrape on her forearm where he had drawn blood. But they were nothing compared to the sharp-pronged pain forking its way between her legs. She wanted to clean herself with warm water.

The steward stepped out. His moustache was twitching. Balanced on one of his palms were her heels, arranged with such care, standing up, agape and waiting for her feet to slide into them. 'Madam, there is nobody there.'

'But…' Anita paused, remembering the way Avinash had greeted the steward. She felt a pulse of anger. 'I'm going to call the police. I'm going to call them right now.'

Immediately his manner changed. Apologetic, he placed the shoes neatly by her feet and raised his hands. 'No need, Madam, no need.' He unclipped a small walkie-talkie from his belt and radioed security. His words blurred into meaningless sounds as she sat on the floor. One of her ankles was swollen, a bruise blossoming around the joint. Her shoulder blades, the bones in her back, they were all inflamed. She reached for her phone and dialled Bharat's number.

The steward once again said, 'No need, madam, no need. I have alerted security.'

She looked up at the man. His skin was dark, his moustache trim, and of all things, he kept nodding his head, as though to reassure her. 'I am calling my brother. Can I do that at least?'

A crease wrinkled his forehead before he said, 'Of course, madam.'

She dialled. When Bharat answered, voice hazy from marijuana, Anita smelt coconut on her hands, her arms, felt fingers scissor her body, and she dropped her phone. She descended the marble stairs of the building, ignoring the calls of the steward asking her to wait. She would not wait. She would not return.

Bikram Sharma is from Bangalore, India. He received his BA in English and Creative Writing from the University of Illinois at Urbana-Champaign before working as an editor. He was awarded UEA's 2014/15 Asian Bursary and is currently working on a novel and a collection of short stories. His writing has appeared or is forthcoming in various literary magazines including *Conifers*, *Bartleby Snopes*, *The Affair*, and *Helter Skelter*.

TATIANA STRAUSS

Blue Speedwell

Novel extract.

I T WAS ALL THE GIANT PULLEY-TYPE THINGS AND STRANGE MACHINERY painted in thick yellows and blues that came first, riding high on the front of the ship, hijacking the best spot like it was more important than all us people paying to get to Fishguard; they looked kind of blobby and like those fancy Lego pieces you get to add reality to your brick-made rockets and tractors and things. I suppose that ferry-boat junk was important, but I didn't care, I was riled; my right to stick myself at the very tip of the water-slicing prow was stolen away.

Not that I wanted to be one of those figurehead girls on the front of the ship, nothing stupid like that.

What I wanted was to be lost in the atmosphere, to be absorbed into the elements of wind and ocean; I wanted to be outside of myself. And bigger. Bigger than my life and all the messed-up stuff of it. To get away from being told what to do and where to go and who I could see.

And I realised that all that rubbish I'd told him, about being made up of the same stuff as nature and everything, that first day on the Irish moor, I realised it was true.

The best I could do was go along a metal walkway down the side of the ship with a million nipples of non-grip grippy-things digging into my white plimsolls and making me slip all over the place. I leant over the guardrail. Everything was freezing to the touch. On tiptoe I extended my vision across the dark curve of the hull, at last got to feel I was forging into the open ocean.

We rose up and plunged down. A fine misty drizzle came at me, smacked my face in irregular rhythms.

I let it slowly soak into my every pore, right through my vest and my cut-offs, puddling in my canvas shoes; felt myself gasping at the sting and the cold, pushed myself further into it. My long hair was so wet it fell heavy, sticking to my face and throat, plastering my scalp.

I wasn't sure if it was actually raining or whether it was the splashed-up spray that was hitting me. Or both. Licking my lips, I found them salty. And I looked down, right into the frothing, surging sea, saw a wide arc of white droplets rise up, then come crashing into me with a rushing sound.

Breaking and coming together again, the way only liquid can.

Every part of me wanted to get lost: lift myself into a handstand on the sopping handrail and somersault off, eyes closed, to meet the swell.

As something touched me from behind, fright leapt in my chest. It was my sister, wide-eyed, staring at me. I laughed, short and shrill, then fell serious, gazing at her through salt-bleared eyes. I couldn't make out what she was saying. She looked impatient. It was clear she resented the pummelling cold and having to come and find me and I realised she was insisting I come inside. But I just stood there, dumb.

And then she was shouting, her face all messed up and reddening.

I nodded quickly, and when she got a hold of my arm, I didn't resist, just let her lead me along the slippery deck. We stepped over the sheet-metal of the raised doorway, through the rubber-edged hole. The oval door was held open by a large rust-laced clip, its peeling paint covered in a sheen of moisture.

'What the hell's the matter with you?' my sister was saying. 'You're such a brat sometimes. Just because you're going home. You had a good time, didn't you? Can't that be enough?'

I smiled wanly, staring down at the blue and red diamond-patterned carpet as we trudged up the stairs and reached the upper deck.

'You should be glad to get away from all that weird talk.'

Her friend was waiting at a table, minding our bags. 'What were you doing?' she said. 'You look like a drowned rat.'

'She was hanging over the side of the ship,' my sister told her. And to me, she said, 'Idiot.' But she gave me a smile that showed she cared, her eyes going soft. 'Didn't want to leave the horses, huh?' She was unzipping her purple nylon sausage bag, extracting a grubby pink towel. 'Here,' she said, passing it to me. 'Dry your hair for a start. Why didn't you wear your coat?' She turned to her friend, said, so I could hear, 'She always does things for attention. Likes danger, huh? Don't you?'

I tipped up my head, rubbed roughly at my hair and scalp.

'Don't you?' she said again, sort of laughing.

I wheeled round with the stinky towel still over my head, hands reaching out like monster claws, made some kind of deep groan. I could see her browned knees sticking out of her flowery skirt and I lurched into her. She shrieked. Her friend burst out laughing and then we were all laughing and it was nice.

'I got you a cake,' my sister said, as she slid along the black vinyl banquette. I slipped in beside her, my skin sticking to the plastic. 'A Chelsea bun. Your favourite.' She passed it to me on a scratched-up industrial plate. 'Here,' she said, delivering a squat cup and saucer of tea, which chattered and splashed and tinkled with the spoon as I took it and put it down in front of me.

'Oh,' I said at the sight of the milky brew.

'What?'

I thought better of it, smiled. 'Nothing. Thank you.' I had only last week given up milk in my tea, and I supposed she'd forgotten.

I knew my sister was looking after me, had been told to keep an eye.

Gazing into the soft spool of dough that was the Chelsea bun, into its sticky, bronze-glazed spiral dotted with currents, I began to unravel it, peeling away its outer layer.

We were in a café, and beyond the ancient window glass, the rolling heathland of County Cork cast its blanket of tufted green, lush with memories of what we did there. Out of sight of others. My hands hugged a mug of black tea with its filmy reflection of distorted shapes and the muted, drizzle-patterned light. As he came over, carrying our second helping of coiled buns, my eye went to him, eating up his burly maleness. I smiled at him without showing my teeth, pretending like I was cool inside.

When he handed me my Chelsea bun, we deliberately brushed fingers and the energy of his touch travelled all the way down to right between my legs. I let him see the spark in my eye.

'Shhh,' he said. I saw he looked kind of nervous.

'What?'

The smile I gave him was innocent. But contained all our secrets and more.

'You're too much,' he told me in a whisper. 'But what an angel face.' As he sat down, he flicked his sights over the room, the people. 'Now stop it.'

'Stop what?' I said, and laughed, cupping my chin as I leaned my elbow onto the red Formica table. I watched his large square hands, loving the wiry black hairs that sprang from the first phalange of each finger. I liked that word. Phalange. It could be anything, I thought. Phalange. Phalange. Phalange. It could be rude. It could be a water bird. A wild flower.

He took up his bun and tore off a strip.

How I wished for his hands to be on me. I envisaged him lying below me, me astride his narrow hips, knees in the grass, crushing blue speedwell, the flesh of me squidging between his fingers, nails digging in.

He put the piece of dough into his mouth and I imagined putting my tongue there, in his mouth, and my lips.

'I want to go,' I said.

'I know. Eat your bun like a good girl.'

'Can't we take them away, our tea and cakes?'

He indicated the landscape through the wavy glass with his head. 'Still raining,' he said.

There was an elastic band in my pocket, I was absently fiddling with it, and I took it out, strained the flesh-coloured fibre between my forefingers, aiming it at him. He watched me. I flicked it. It hit him in the face. He didn't flinch.

'You're such a kid,' he said.

'I am a kid. What the fuck did you say that for?'

He shrugged, picked up the elastic band, caught an edge of it in his mouth, under an eye tooth, and kept pinging it against his lip. My sights grazed his craggy face, refused his blue eyes. He put the rubber band in his pocket, took a sip of my black tea; black like his, but mine; he took a sip.

'Hey,' he murmured, leaning forward. 'I know you're not a kid. What you are, is – don't you know? You're everything.'

I could smell him and it threw me and I flinched.

The ferry lurched, like it was hit by a huge wave at a funny angle.

My tea slopped over the side of my cup, spilled over the saucer and splashed my bare leg. It was tepid and rather pleasant, like warm fingers. I was eating the bun right up to my mouth, nuzzling at its entrails in one continuous consummation.

'You're disgusting,' my sister said. 'Anyone would think you were five, eating like that – not fourteen.'

I grinned, still with the bun in my face. I said, 'No one thinks I'm five.'

'You know what I mean.'

'I don't actually.'

She tried not to laugh. 'I think you were put on this earth especially to get on my nerves.'

'No, to teach you,' I told her, as I stuffed the last bit of bun in my gob. I tried not to think of chips, of his fingers mashing them into my mouth, down on the quay, that day, before we did it for the first time.

My sister gasped, all theatrical, and was laughing and saying something about how it was her job to teach me, older is wiser, experience is knowledge, something like that.

I wondered what she would think if she realised just how experienced I was. I wondered if she would hate me for lying to her. And for getting there before she did.

And then I swear I could smell him, like he was there. I had to take a quick glance behind me to check. And I thought I heard the scream of a seagull, my eyes drawn to the window, frantically in search of it, remembering the chips I'd thrown on the water and the gulls diving in and fighting each other for them.

'Was that a gull?' I said.

I didn't know why at the time, but obviously I seemed stupid.

'Not a seagull!' her friend squawked.

This sent my sister off, and her friend too, the two of them wrapping their arms around themselves, clutching their sides. Laughter rippled through me despite myself. I realised I was blinking a lot and that tears were spilling out of me. I wanted to howl. So I copied them, bent over double, wiped at my eyes. It was easier that way.

An itinerant childhood saw **Tatiana Strauss** attend eleven different schools, moving from London to Wales, then East Anglia, before returning to London and becoming an actress. She formed Living Theatre, co-writing *Bloodsuckers*, a tale of sibling incest, which was performed in London and Paris. She then wrote and directed her award-winning feature film, *Space Invader*.

ROWAN WHITESIDE

White-Coated Vultures

This is an extract from a novel-in-progress,
provisionally entitled Heartsick.

Ellie isn't supposed to die yet: she's only twenty-two. But her car collided with
a lamppost, the doctors have declared her brain-dead, and her parents have
agreed to donate her organs – Ellie's objections don't come into the matter.
Ellie finds herself tied to those who received her organs, forced to experience
their lives due to a quirk of flesh and blood.

ERIN THE SOCIAL WORKER COMES CLIP-CLOPPING ALONG THE WARD
floor. She peers round the curtain corner, her bob slicing a sharp
shadow on her neck. 'How are you guys doing?'

Oh, just hunky dory, thanks Erin. My parents think I'm dead and
have decided to switch me off and recycle the parts, and I'm some sort
of ineffectual sprite whose only method of communication is giving
someone the goosebumps.

My dad shifts in his seat. 'Can we talk to the nurse—'

My mother breaks in: 'Abigail.'

'Yes. Could we talk to Abigail please?'

I'm torn between sitting shiva with my body and following my
parents to watch them sign my life away.

I wonder if the slip of paper I signed is stored somewhere, the red
print faded, my signature still standing black. It could be stuffed into a
filing cabinet in a basement (next to all the other Clarkes), or stacked in
a box along with the other official fragments of my life: birth certificate,
medical records, exam certificates, driving licence, student loan debts.

It's more likely that some minimum-wage government employee
ticked a box on a computer screen and my assent got spirited away to

a database, coded into meaningless strings of symbols and letters. My signature was probably shredded into hamster bedding curls, sliced into unrecognisable fragments and wrapped in a polythene bag with other people's promises.

A signature on its own means nothing.

Someone's left the door of the Nurses' Station open and I can see my parents nodding as the nurse speaks. Billy's staring at the floor and digging clenched fists into his stomach.

I turn, stare at the monitor, trying to make sense of the lines and numbers. My heartbeat is plodding, artificially slow. I look from the screen to my body, adding the two together and losing the answer, then move down and press myself onto my chest.

I think of the other times I've counted heartbeats, sated and sticky on someone else's skin, playing doctors with a plastic stethoscope, counting extra slow to a hundred before a game of hide and seek, accelerating as the pressure builds.

Panic rises inside me, but my breath doesn't stir, my heartbeat doesn't quicken. It makes no change to my body, how I'm feeling.

Maybe this is supposed to happen, maybe people just get cast out from their bodies moments before their death, maybe this is how it is meant to be. But I haven't seen anybody, or sensed them, or anything. And surely a hospital would be crammed with severed souls, packed to the brim with the imminently or recently deceased?

There's the morgue, line after line of flat still bodies, chilled into acceptance. The wards filled with the sick and dying, bodies and minds split as the heartbeat stops: as the blood pools with a drip drip drip, a knife slips, a pillow is pressed down, a screaming bloodied mother, a flopping empty child, a small clot slipping, too many pills swallowed, a sharp corner, a long sickness, a cancerous cell, an extra drop of morphine sweetheart, some sort of infection (they think), a drunken snort of something that was supposed to be coke, a fight on a Friday night. So many ways to die.

I look back at my family, at the nurse. I can see Abigail's lips moving. I bet she's telling them that I won't feel a thing. That's what they always say, isn't it? It's the kindest way, it won't hurt a bit, it's for the best, they won't suffer this way. Like I'm a cat that's been run over, cowering in my cage, about to have my fur parted and a thin needle inserted.

I stare at my body in disgust. It might not feel a thing, but I'm pretty sure I will. I'll have to watch my body sliced up, a piece of meat on a butcher's slab, or I'll fade away as they cut out my organs one by one, and everything will just stop as they pick my heart out of my chest.

I poke myself again, hard above my right breast, then move towards the open door. Abigail's speaking: 'The operation – it'll save so many lives. It's no compensation, of course, but it's a little bit of hope.'

I wish I'd been given the hope, rather than having it parcelled away in a perverse Pandora's box.

Enough. Like I need to hear about how my death is going to be beneficial to strangers, why my tragedy is someone else's miracle.

I touch the box charting my body and thrust my hand through the screen. The glass doesn't shatter and the display barely flickers. I trace a wire behind the box, following the snake down to the bottom, feel the stubby joint of the cord and learn its heft, before focusing myself at it one hard urge.

The lights dim almost imperceptibly and my box starts to beep. I look down at my body, suddenly reminded that it's only functioning due to the pulse of a machine.

A nurse walks over, her thin-soled shoes scuffing at the floor, and presses a few buttons so the noise stops. I watch my life displayed in another language, reduced to its most cursory summary.

'There we go, much better.' She peers down at my body, then tucks the sheets in around my shoulders.

Abigail holds the door wide and my family file out one by one. My mother's eyes are red-rimmed, and she's holding my father's hand.

The nurse glances at my family then turns back to me. 'They'll come back and see you before you go, don't worry.'

There's a collection of white-coated vultures cluttering up my bedside. They're discussing the options for my organs, the viability of my flesh. I'm on the bed alongside my body; the folded shadow settled next to my skull, an unknown spectator.

'Do you think her parents might agree to donate her brain?' It's a girl speaking, with close-cropped hair and a glistening nose piercing. She looks too eager to please, poised to reveal her sheath of top-notch qualifications. 'Only they're doing some fascinating research on schizophrenia down at Queen's and I know they're looking for control samples.'

I don't want my brain to bob in a bottle, its whorls and creases on display for everyone to see. I don't want it to be shaved into Carpaccio and served on a slide. I want my brain to stay safe in my skull, swollen sides pressed against solid bone, wedged intact at the start of my spine.

I don't want my body to become an experiment for undergraduates, my breasts to be rated out of ten, my eyeballs to be cut open. I don't want to lie on a metal gurney for months, wheeled out on weekdays to be cut and prodded and ineptly carved. Everybody knows that med students are not to be trusted.

The medical students were the ones to avoid back at uni. They'd gather at The Shift, drunk and raving in lab coats, pouring booze down their throats and chanting mnemonics, picking up girls to practise anatomy on: rollicking already, inflated with the promise of power over life.

Leave my brain alone, bitch.

The doctor in charge tips his glasses down his nose and peers at the girl: 'Let's just concentrate on the job at hand.'

I cheer him on, my new balding ally.

'An organ harvesting is an unfortunately rare event, so it is of the utmost importance that the family doesn't change their mind.'

Traitor.

'Our transplant nurse, Abigail, will co-ordinate with other hospitals to find suitable recipients.'

I picture a lucky dip; the slowly-dying in hanging hospital gowns queuing in front of a barrel, ready to sink their hand into the sawdust and pull out a gift-wrapped hunk of meat.

The bald doctor turns, 'I'd recommend that you all take the opportunity to observe this operation,' he says, walking away without looking back, his flock of students following obediently.

I hadn't realised my death was a spectator sport.

The grey dawn is filtering through the blinds, turning the now empty ward into a dimly lit set. Bodies bulge under sheets, still apart from the slow rise and fall of chests. I move to the foot of my bed and examine the clipboard fastened to the edge of the frame. I can't read the handwriting.

I reach for the clipboard, intending to tilt the page to see if it makes the writing more legible, but it's like I'm trying to capture fog in my hands: impossible. I pull myself closer to the chart, try to make sense of the scrawl and the strings of numbers, but it's nonsense, gobbledygook: a foreign language of abbreviations and symbols.

I will my neurons to knit together, for the spindly fringes to reach and connect and spark. I shrink my swollen tissue down; let the blood carry oxygen around my brain. I watch each section slowly glow, each cortex brighten. I feel myself back into my body, suddenly whole, ready to take full advantage of my precious flesh, ready to run and skip and conquer. I stretch, splay my fingers, point my toes, pull my spine.

My body stays still.

I itch to squeeze the tube full of air tight shut, to close my body off from oxygen: a short sharp shock, like turning it off and on again, an attempt to restore my body to its factory settings. I feel as if I'm tightrope walking along a steep sharp drop, tempted to throw myself over the edge even as I command my legs to walk away, not to take that extra teasing step into nothingness.

My parents still haven't arrived.

I'm beginning to think they're not going to come at all, that they've decided it will be too traumatic to say another goodbye, that they're already busy booking the funeral parlour and packing away my clothes and spreading the news.

I can't believe Mum didn't stay with me. When I get ill she always tells me to come home, to let her look after me, that I'll heal quicker if she's on hand to dose me and feed me and check my temperature. But now I really need her and she's just left me here, another length of human carrion.

I wish they'd left me to die in my car. I'd rather my last breath had been tinged with diesel instead of this disinfected air. I wonder if they could bronze the car, place my corpse inside, leave it as a crumpled statue in memoriam. I'd prefer that to a bench.

The accident's a blur of smoke and pain. It wasn't my fault, I know it wasn't my fault, the light was green. Green for go, green for life, green for safety. I think the other car was red, a bright shade of danger coming fast towards me, but maybe the blood was already colouring my view.

Rowan Whiteside was born in South Africa but has lived primarily in the UK. She completed a BA in English and American Literature at UEA. Her writing has been published online on various sites, and in print in the first *Words and Women* Anthology. Find her on Twitter *@DilysTolfree*.